IMPACTS OF BORDER ENFORCEMENT ON MEXICAN MIGRATION

Central plaza in Tlacuitapa, Jalisco. Photograph by Wayne Cornelius.

IMPACTS OF BORDER ENFORCEMENT ON MEXICAN MIGRATION

THE VIEW FROM SENDING COMMUNITIES

edited by

Wayne A. Cornelius and Jessa M. Lewis

CCIS Anthologies, No. 3

LA JOLLA, CALIFORNIA

CENTER FOR COMPARATIVE IMMIGRATION STUDIES, UCSD

ISBN-13: 978-0-9702838-7-0 (paper)
ISBN-10: 0-9702838-7-3 (paper)
ISBN-13: 978-0-9702838-6-3 (cloth)
ISBN-10: 0-9702838-6-5 (cloth)
Printed in the United States of America

Library of Congress Cataloging-in-Publication Data

Impacts of border enforcement on Mexican migration : the view from sending communities / edited by Wayne A. Cornelius and Jessa M. Lewis.
    p. cm. -- (CCIS anthologies ; no. 3)
  Includes bibliographical references.
  ISBN 978-0-9702838-7-0 (pbk.) -- ISBN 978-0-9702838-6-3 (cloth) 1. United States--Emigration and immigration. 2. Illegal aliens--Government policy--United States. 3. Border patrols--Mexican-American Border Region. 4. Mexico--Emigration and immigration. 5. Mexicans--United States. I. Cornelius, Wayne A., 1945- II. Lewis, Jessa M. III. Title. IV. Series.

HV6483.I46 2007
325'.2720973--dc22

CONTENTS

ACKNOWLEDGMENTS

The research on which this book is based was supported by generous grants from the Ford Foundation, the Tinker Foundation, and the Metropolis Project/Foundation for Population, Migration, and Environment. Additional support was provided by Eleanor Roosevelt College, the Center for the Study of Race and Ethnicity, and the Senior Vice Chancellor at the University of California, San Diego.

Rodolfo García Zamora and his graduate students at the Universidad Autónoma de Zacatecas ably conducted field interviewing for the Zacatecas component of the study. At UCSD, essential contributions to the project were made by Jessa M. Lewis, Graduate Teaching Assistant for the Mexican Migration Field Research and Training Program, and Graduate Research Assistants Luis Estrada, Idean Salehyan, and Scott Borger.

Our greatest debt is owed to the people of Tlacuitapa, Jalisco, and Las Ánimas, Zacatecas, whose cooperation and active engagement with the research was extraordinary. We hope that this book faithfully reflects their experiences as migrants to the United States as well as their struggles to better themselves and their communities.

1

Introduction: Does Border Enforcement Deter Unauthorized Immigration?

WAYNE A. CORNELIUS

Recent U.S. policy for controlling "unwanted" immigration has been based on a key premise: most illegal entries could be deterred by strengthening enforcement along the 2,000-mile U.S.-Mexico border. The last thirteen years have brought a step-level increase in Border Patrol resources, manpower, and technology, aimed at preventing the entry of undocumented migrants from Mexico (and nationals of other countries crossing the Mexican border). Enhanced border enforcement efforts promised to decrease the probability of persons entering undetected and evading apprehension, thereby lowering the expected benefits of migration. But has stronger border enforcement affected the propensity of individual Mexicans to migrate illegally?

In addition, the evidence suggests that since the initiation of "Operation Gatekeeper" in the San Diego sector and similar concentrated border enforcement initiatives, the risk of death and injury as a consequence of clandestine entry has increased sharply, along with the fees that professional people-smugglers charge for their services. Are potential migrants aware of these heightened risks and costs, and does such knowledge discourage them from migrating without papers? Or do the powerful economic and family-related incentives that traditionally have driven Mexican migration to the United States outweigh these considerations? If they opt to go north, what border-crossing strategies do unauthorized migrants use to reduce their risk and increase the probability of successful entry?

Jessa Lewis and Idean Salehyan contributed valuable research assistance for this chapter.

POLICING THE U.S.-MEXICO BORDER

Since 1993 the U.S. government has been seriously committed to reducing the flow of unauthorized immigration from Mexico through tougher border enforcement. The operational strategy pursued by the Border Patrol during this period has been to concentrate enforcement resources along four heavily transited segments of the border, from San Diego in the west to the South Rio Grande Valley in the east. The logic of this "concentrated border enforcement" strategy is simple: illegal crossings will be deterred by forcing entries to be made in the remote, hazardous areas between the highly fortified segments of the border.

Approximately 75 miles of sturdy metal fencing were erected to prevent crossings in urban areas where illegal entry was most visible. In addition, there has been a remarkable increase in the sophistication of surveillance and apprehension technology, including remote video surveillance systems, infrared monitors, seismic sensors that can detect footsteps, helicopters, unmanned aerial vehicles (drones), and computerized databases. The number of Border Patrol agents rose from 3,965 in September 1993 to 11,106 in September 2005, and total spending on border enforcement grew sixfold during this period. Since Fiscal Year 2002, the growth in spending has outpaced increases in apprehensions being made at the border (see figure 1.1).

Under the Border Patrol's doctrine of "prevention through deterrence," it was believed that by significantly increasing apprehension rates and the visibility of the Border Patrol, potential migrants would be dissuaded from attempting a crossing. In testimony before the U.S. House of Representatives, the late Barbara Jordan, chair of the congressionally mandated U.S. Commission on Immigration Reform, offered an apt summary of this doctrine: "It is far better to *deter* illegal immigration than to play the cat and mouse game that results from apprehensions followed by return followed by re-entry. To accomplish a true *deterrence* strategy will require additional personnel as well as a strategic use of technology and equipment" (House of Representatives, March 29, 1995, italics added).

The post-1993 border enforcement strategy has raised the probability of apprehension on any given trip to the border, which was the explicitly stated aim of government officials when the strategy was being planned. For example, from Fiscal Year 2002 to Fiscal Year 2004, each unauthorized migrant detained by the Border Patrol had been apprehended 1.38 times on average. Two years later, the average migrant had been apprehended 1.57 times (see table 1.1). This trend has been interpreted by immigration authorities as evidence of the efficacy of the concentrated border enforcement strategy, but that would be so only if repeat crossers were being discouraged after multiple apprehensions and returning to their places of origin. There is, however, no evidence that the higher probability of apprehension in heavily fortified corridors is having such an effect on migrants' behavior. The vast majority of apprehended migrants attempt to enter again the next evening or within a couple of days. People-smugglers typically give their clients three "free" tries, and most do not need more than one or two (Cornelius 1998: 130; Sherry 2004; Spener 2001).

Rather than create a systematic, borderwide deterrent effect, concentrated enforcement operations seem only to have redistributed illegal entries. Migrants and the people-smugglers who assist them have just detoured around the heavily fortified segments of the border. A rapid decline in apprehensions in the first-fortified El Paso and San Diego areas was accompanied by increases in apprehensions along unfortified segments of the border in Arizona, New Mexico, and Texas (Bean et al. 1994; Cornelius 2001). By 2006, the crackdown on illegal entries through Arizona that began in the late 1990s had pushed the migrant traffic back toward San Diego and El Paso, sectors that had been declared "operationally controlled" by the Border Patrol (Cornelius 2006).

Moreover, the post-1993 border enforcement buildup has had several important unintended consequences. First, while urban areas—such as San Diego, Calexico, Nogales, and El Paso—witnessed the building of physical barriers and the deployment of many more Border Patrol agents, remote areas in the mountains and deserts along the border were left largely unfortified. This has led migrants to attempt riskier crossings through more remote and hazardous terrain; consequently, the risk of death or injury has increased sharply in recent years (Cornelius 2001, 2005). Between 1995 and 2006, there were over 3,700 *known* migrant fatalities due to unauthorized border crossings; dehydration and hypothermia were the most common causes of death. The

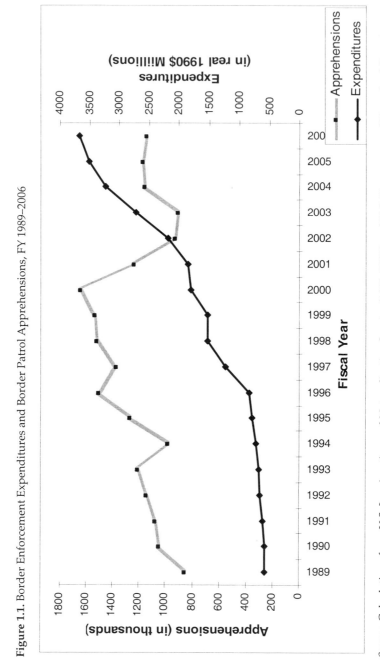

Figure 1.1. Border Enforcement Expenditures and Border Patrol Apprehensions, FY 1989–2006

Source: Calculations from U.S. Immigration and Naturalization Service (1989–2002) and U.S. Department of Homeland Security (2003–2006) data.

actual death toll undoubtedly was much higher, including bodies yet undiscovered.

Second, while unassisted crossings were previously common, more and more migrants have turned to professional people-smugglers (known by the migrants as *"coyotes"* or *"polleros"*) to assist them in clandestine entry. *Coyotes* are hired to lead migrants through difficult crossing areas, provide fraudulent identity documents, and pass migrants through legal ports of entry using false or borrowed documents (Spener 2001, 2005). As the demand for their services increased with tighter border enforcement, people-smugglers tripled or quadrupled their fees. Use of *coyotes* has become the unauthorized migrant's principal strategy for reducing physical risk and increasing the probability of successful entry.

Table 1.1. Border Patrol Apprehensions and Individuals Apprehended, FY 2002–2004

	FY 2002	FY 2003	FY 2004
(a) Apprehensions	955,310	931,557	1,159,802
(b) Individuals	693,798	638,480	741,115
Recidivism rate: (a)/(b)	1.38	1.46	1.57

Sources: U.S. Department of Homeland Security, Border Patrol Enforcement Integrated Database; Winograd 2004; calculations by the author.

Finally, there is growing evidence that tighter border enforcement in the post-1993 period has lengthened the U.S. sojourns of unauthorized migrants and increased their probability of settling permanently in the United States. Both legal and illegal migrants were staying longer in the United States in the late 1990s, but the sojourns of unauthorized migrants were especially extended.[1] In 1992, about 20 percent of Mexico-to-U.S. migrants returned home after six months; in 1997 about 15 percent did, and by 2000 only 7 percent of migrants did so (Reyes, Johnson, and Swearingen 2002). According to another estimate, based on data

---

[1] Encuesta sobre Migración en la Frontera Norte de México (EMIF), El Colegio de la Frontera Norte, Consejo Nacional de Población, Secretaría de Trabajo y Previsión Social, Instituto Nacional de Migración, 7 Fases (1993–2002).

from migrant-sending communities, the likelihood that an undocu-mented migrant will return to Mexico within a year after entry into the United States fell from 45 percent in the early 1980s to about 25 percent (Massey 2006; Massey, Durand, and Malone 2002: 128–33; see also Reyes 2004). Another important indicator of the reduced circularity in Mexico-to-U.S. migration is robust growth in the stock of unauthorized migrants living in the United States, which has more than doubled during the era of tighter border enforcement (Passel 2006). Because each return trip to the United States now costs thousands of dollars in *coyote* fees and exposes the migrant to life-threatening hazards, millions of unauthorized migrants apparently have opted to remain on the U.S. side of the border indefinitely.

Previous research has shown that migration decisions by Mexicans without papers are a function of several factors; relative wages, social network contacts, the probability of successful entry, the risk of physi-cal harm, and *coyote* fees are all taken into account (Durand and Massey 2004; Sherry 2004). In theory, potential migrants should be deterred by the additional costs and risks created by the U.S. border enforcement strategy, but with expected earnings in the United States often eight to ten times higher than in Mexico, labor market forces and family ties to the United States could offset the heightened risks and costs of clandes-tine border crossings. It is this complex interplay of border enforce-ment–related variables and traditional drivers of unauthorized migra-tion from Mexico to the United States that we sought to illuminate through the field research reported in this volume.

RESEARCH DESIGN AND METHODOLOGY

The study collected individual and community-level data that enable us to establish direct linkages between changes in immigration control policies and changes (or lack of change) in migrants' behavior. Types of behavior studied include the decision to migrate internationally, the timing of such decisions, the migrant's choice of destination, mode of entry (including, in the case of unauthorized migrants, the choice be-tween unassisted entry and reliance on professional smugglers), and participation in a possible temporary worker program. The data gath-ered for this study constitute the most detailed and direct evidence of the failure of the post-1993 U.S. border enforcement strategy to deter unauthorized entries, and suggest some of the reasons for this failure of deterrence.

This study was undertaken as the inaugural project of the Mexican Migration Field Research and Training Program, established in 2004 as a joint activity of the Center for Comparative Immigration Studies and Eleanor Roosevelt College at the University of California, San Diego.[2] The program seeks to train new generations of students—undergraduates and graduate students, U.S. and Mexican citizens—to become proficient field researchers in international migration studies. Another goal is to generate new, individual-level datasets on Mexican migration that can be used to address key issues of public policy and developments of concern in both the United States and Mexico. The field research sites as well as the substantive foci of the research vary from year to year. Each year's project is undertaken under the joint auspices of the University of California, San Diego and a Mexican partner university, whose faculty and students participate in the questionnaire construction and field interviewing (for the project reported in this volume, that partner was the Universidad Autónoma de Zacatecas).

Sending community–based survey research on Mexico-to-U.S. migration has been done since 1975,[3] and it has proven to be an essential methodology for transcending the limits of national-level census and other official datasets in studying Mexican migration, particularly unauthorized flows. Our program uses a quasi-longitudinal methodology, in which the same, purposively selected migrant-sending communities are restudied every two or three years.[4] This type of design is optimal

---

[2] For a detailed description of the program, see http://www.polisci.ucsd.edu/cornelius/.

[3] The pioneering project was a comparative study of nine rural communities in the region of Los Altos de Jalisco, conducted in 1975–1976 by Wayne Cornelius and collaborating researchers at the Universidad de Guadalajara (see Cornelius 1976). For a review of subsequent sending community–based research on Mexican migration to the United States, see Jones 1995: 10–14. Durand and Massey (2004) provide a synthesis of sending-community research conducted under the auspices of their Mexican Migration Project since 1982.

[4] The design is "quasi-longitudinal" because the same respondents may or may not be reinterviewed in different years. However, given the small size of the

for documenting and explaining changes in U.S.-bound migration patterns, especially those resulting from changes in U.S. immigration law and policy, as well as for observing how migrant-sending communities are being transformed economically and culturally by emigration and flows of migrant remittances, human capital, and information.

Each of our field studies includes both standardized survey interviews and longer, semi-structured, "life history" interviews. The life history interviews, which are digitally recorded and transcribed, enable us to gather more fine-grained information about migration and employment experiences in the United States and Mexico that helps in interpreting the standardized survey interview data. They also enable us to explore issues that cannot be covered in sufficient detail in the standardized questionnaire. In the books resulting from our program, extensive information from life history interviews is integrated into the discussion of data from the standardized survey interviews.

Our 2004–2005 project generated a survey dataset on 603 returned migrants and potential first-time migrants to the United States. They were interviewed in January 2005 in two rural communities with high rates of emigration. These communities are located, respectively, in Jalisco and Zacatecas—states that traditionally have been among the leading sources of migrants to the United States. These communities were chosen purposively to take advantage of extensive baseline data from previous surveys of migration behavior conducted in these towns. Tlacuitapa, Jalisco, had been the site of surveys in 1976, 1988–1989, and 1995 (see Cornelius 1976, 1991, 1998). Las Ánimas, Zacatecas, had been studied in 1980 (Mines 1981) and 1988–1989 (Cornelius 1991; Goldring 1991, 1992).

In addition to the 603 standardized survey interviews conducted in the two towns, life history interviews were done with a subsample of 28 returned migrants. These interviewees were selected based on information they provided during administration of the standardized questionnaire. The average administration time for the standardized questionnaire was 50 minutes; the life histories could range from one to

---

research communities, we expect the samples interviewed in successive years to contain many of the same individuals and/or their relatives.

three hours, given their open-ended character. The standardized questionnaire and life history interviews were supplemented by other in-
depth interviews with key informants (priest, doctor, municipal government delegate, factory manager, and so on) in the research communities.

The standardized questionnaire was administered to at least one
adult in every dwelling unit that was occupied during the fieldwork
period. Due to the small populations of the research communities, no
sampling was necessary. In each dwelling, the interviewer was instructed first to interview the male head of household. If the male head
of household was unavailable throughout the fieldwork period, interviewers were instructed to interview his wife about her husband's migration experiences. If at that time the wife volunteered that she had
migration experience of her own, she was interviewed concerning her
migration experience as well.[5] After interviewing the head of household, the questionnaire was next administered to all sons and daughters of at least 15 years of age. We administered the standardized questionnaire only to people aged 15 to 65, since we expected to find the
majority of current and potential migrants in this age range.

In the process of surveying the towns, numerous unoccupied or
totally abandoned houses were discovered. In Tlacuitapa, the number
of abandoned homes had increased notably since the 1995 survey conducted there, suggesting that the long-standing tradition of emigration
from this community is evolving toward permanent settlement in the
United States. The research team kept records of these abandoned
houses and attempted to document what had happened to the residents
of the unoccupied homes by asking neighbors.

Of the 437 persons interviewed in Tlacuitapa and the 166 persons
interviewed in Las Ánimas, 68 percent were categorized by interviewers as having their principal base in the sending community, while 31
percent were based primarily in the United States and were making
short visits to their hometown at the time of our fieldwork. Six percent
of all respondents were U.S.-born citizens, and 15 percent were natural-

---

[5] Since female heads of household were not interviewed by default, as males
were, this led to a slight degree of gender bias in our interviewee population.
Chapter 6 in this volume details the impacts of the field interviewing methodology on our analysis of gender differences.

ized U.S. citizens. This, too, reflects the towns' multi-generational tradition of migration to the United States.

The survey questionnaire contained a total of 143 items (see Appendix A). In addition to questions pertaining to basic demographics, the standardized questionnaire contained sections on employment and residency in 2004; the migratory history of the family from 1995 to 2005; the migratory history of the interviewee; intentions to migrate in the 12 months following the interview; employment and life in the United States; perceptions of the interviewee's hometown and his economic situation; and plans for the future. Although the majority of questions were closed, open-ended questions were included to elicit more fine-grained information on various aspects of the migration experience.

The semi-structured life history interviews conducted for this study did not follow any particular format. However, interviewers were equipped with an "interview guide" to ensure coverage of topics particularly relevant to the research objectives (see Appendix B). Particular attention was given in these interviews to recent border-crossing strategies and experiences; experiences while living in the United States; the effects of migration on family life, hometown culture, and development; and civic participation in the sending and receiving communities.

As noted above, interviewers selected life history interviewees on the basis of information provided (and how candidly this information was provided) during administration of the standardized questionnaire. In addition to persons who had migrated to the United States recently, interviewers sought out individuals with long-term migration experience (such as former participants in the "bracero" contract labor program of 1942–1964), who could provide perspective on changes over time in their hometown's migratory profile. The researchers were also encouraged to interview some persons who had *never* migrated to the United States, in order to gain insight into the behavior of these permanent stay-at-homes.

SELECTED FINDINGS

How have heightened border controls affected the decision making of unauthorized Mexican migrants to the United States? Our findings support earlier research showing that tightened border enforcement since 1993 has not stopped, nor even discouraged, unauthorized migrants from entering the United States (see, for example, Orrenius 2004).[6] Our data show that a higher percentage of unauthorized migrants are being apprehended on a given trip to the border than in the 1980s. Even so, only 23 percent of our undocumented interviewees who reported crossing the border during the period of tighter border enforcement since 1993 had been caught even once by the Border Patrol. This indicates that even with an unprecedented level of border enforcement, the vast majority of unauthorized migrants are able to enter without being detected. And even if migrants are caught, they keep trying until they succeed. Our interviews with returned migrants revealed that 92 percent of them eventually succeeded on the same trip to the border, without returning to their place of origin.

We found our interviewees to be well informed about the difficulties of surmounting the obstacle course that has been erected at the border. Seventy-two percent were aware of the post-1993 concentrated border enforcement operations, and a similar proportion believed that it is much more difficult or nearly impossible to evade the Border Patrol. Eight out of ten thought that it is much more dangerous to cross the border without papers today, and nearly two-thirds of our interviewees personally knew someone who had died trying to enter clandestinely. But for the overwhelming majority of potential migrants, such knowledge does not diminish the propensity to go north. Asked whether they intended to migrate at some point during 2005, 51 percent of our interviewees responded affirmatively. And of those not intending to migrate, fewer than one out of five cited border enforcement–related reasons for that choice (including higher *coyote* fees). Family obligations, lack of economic need, and advanced age were the most important impediments to migration.

To evade apprehension by the Border Patrol and to reduce the risks posed by natural hazards, nine out of ten unauthorized migrants from our research communities had hired a *coyote* to assist them on their most recent trip to the United States. We also found that, with clandes-

---

[6] For a more detailed analysis of our data on the effects of U.S. border enforcement on migration behavior, see chapter 4, this volume.

tine border crossing an increasingly expensive and risky business, U.S. border enforcement policy is encouraging many undocumented migrants to remain in the United States for longer periods. Heavier indebtedness to people-smugglers, whose fees have been pushed upward by tighter border controls, is one of the reasons for extended stays. And the longer the sojourn, the greater the likelihood of "settling out" in the United States.

If the post-1993 U.S. border enforcement strategy were working, we should be seeing that the increased costs and risks of clandestine entry are discouraging prospective migrants even from leaving home. However, our analysis reveals that tougher border controls have had remarkably little influence on the decision to migrate to the United States among potential Mexican immigrants. Economic and family-related incentives remain the principal determinants of such decisions. While there is evidence to suggest that migration *strategies* have been affected by enhanced border security—crossing points have changed and the use of people-smugglers has increased—these policies have by and large been ineffective in discouraging clandestine entry attempts. Our data also indicate that migrants who go to the border and are apprehended have an extremely high rate of success if they persist. Despite the border buildup, most unauthorized migrants still succeed in entering on the first or second try.

Our findings suggest that current U.S. immigration control policy is fundamentally flawed. The stated aim of reducing the flow and stock of unauthorized immigrants through a robust deterrence strategy has not been achieved. It is possible that, with significantly higher levels of manpower and new technology, the current strategy may eventually produce some of the anticipated results, but the time frame for effectiveness is highly uncertain. And it is equally possible that ratcheting up investment in this strategy will yield only more of the same unintended consequences that have been observed since 1993—absent a systematic, stringent campaign of workplace enforcement to reduce employer demand for undocumented immigrant labor.

An alternative approach—such as increasing legal entry opportunities for low-skilled foreign workers through a guestworker program and providing a larger number of permanent, employment-based visas for such workers—may have a higher probability of success. In future field studies, the Mexican Migration Field Research and Training Program will explore how this approach could affect migration behavior, as well as development options to create alternatives to emigration in labor-exporting communities.

References

Bean, Frank D., Roland Chanove, Robert G. Cushing, Rodolfo de la Garza, Gary Freeman, Charles W. Haynes, and David Spener. 1994. *Illegal Mexican Migration and the United States/Mexico Border: The Effects of Operation Hold-the-Line on El Paso and Juárez.* Washington, D.C.: U.S. Commission on Immigration Reform.

Cornelius, Wayne A. 1976. "Outmigration from Rural Mexican Communities." In *The Dynamics of Migration: International Migration.* Occasional Monograph Series, Vol. 2, No. 5, ICP Work Agreement Reports. Washington, D.C.: Interdisciplinary Communications Program, Smithsonian Institution.

———. 1991. "Labor Migration to the United States: Development Outcomes and Alternatives in Mexican Sending Communities." In *Regional and Sectoral Development in Mexico as Alternatives to Migration*, ed. Sergio Díaz-Briquets and Sidney Weintraub. Boulder, Colo.: Westview.

———. 1998. "Ejido Reform: Stimulus or Alternative to Migration?" In *The Transformation of Rural Mexico*, ed. Wayne A. Cornelius and David Myhre. La Jolla: Center for U.S.-Mexican Studies, University of California, San Diego.

———. 2001. "Death at the Border: Efficacy and Unintended Consequences of U.S. Immigration Control Policy," *Population and Development Review* 27, no. 4: 661–85.

———. 2005. "Controlling 'Unwanted' Immigration: Lessons from the United States, 1993–2004," *Journal of Ethnic and Migration Studies* 31, no. 4: 775–94.

———. 2006. "Impacts of Border Enforcement on Unauthorized Mexican Migration to the United States," *Border Battles: The U.S. Immigration Debates*, Web Forum of the Social Science Research Council, September, http://borderbattles.ssrc.org/Cornelius/.

Durand, Jorge, and Douglas S. Massey, eds. 2004. *Crossing the Border: Research from the Mexican Migration Project.* New York: Russell Sage Foundation.

Goldring, Luin P. 1991. "Development and Migration: A Comparative Analysis of Two Mexican Migrant Circuits." In *The Effects of Receiving Country Policies on Migration Flows.* Boulder, Colo.: Westview.

———. 1992. "Diversity and Community in Transnational Migration: A Comparative Study of Two Mexico-U.S. Migrant Circuits." PhD dissertation, Cornell University.

Jones, Richard C. 1995. *Ambivalent Journey: U.S. Migration and Economic Mobility in North-Central Mexico.* Tucson, Ariz.: University of Arizona Press.

Massey, Douglas S. 2006. "Borderline Madness," *Chronicle of Higher Education,* June 30.

Massey, Douglas S., Jorge Durand, and Nolan J. Malone. 2002. *Beyond Smoke and Mirrors: Mexican Immigration in an Era of Economic Integration.* New York: Russell Sage Foundation.

Mines, Richard. 1981. *Developing a Community Tradition of Migration: A Field Study in Rural Zacatecas, Mexico, and California Settlement Areas.* Monograph No. 3. La Jolla: Center for U.S.-Mexican Studies, University of California, San Diego.

Orrenius, P. M. 2004. "The Effect of U.S. Border Enforcement on the Crossing Behavior of Mexican Migrants." In *Crossing the Border: Research from the Mexican Migration Project,* ed. Jorge Durand and Douglas S. Massey. New York: Russell Sage Foundation.

Passel, Jeffrey. 2006. "Size and Characteristics of the Unauthorized Migrant Population in the United States: Estimates Based on the March 2005 Current Population Survey." Washington, D.C.: Pew Hispanic Center, March 7, http://pewhispanic.org/reports/report.php?ReportID=61.

Reyes, Belinda. 2004. "U.S. Immigration Policy and the Duration of Undocumented Trips." In *Crossing the Border: Research from the Mexican Migration Project,* ed. Jorge Durand and Douglas S. Massey. New York: Russell Sage Foundation.

Reyes, Belinda, Hans P. Johnson, and R. V. Swearingen. 2002. *Holding the Line?—The Effect of the Recent Border Build-up on Unauthorized Immigration.* San Francisco, Calif.: Public Policy Institute of California.

Sherry, Adam. 2004. "Foundations of U.S. Immigration Control Policy: A Study of Information Transmission to Mexican Migrants." CCIS Working Paper No. 95. La Jolla: Center for Comparative Immigration Studies, University of California, San Diego, http://www.ccis-ucsd.org/PUBLICATIONS/wrkg95.pdf.

Spener, David. 2001. "Smuggling Migrants through South Texas: Challenges Posed by Operation Rio Grande." In *Global Human Smuggling: Comparative Perspectives*, ed. David Kyle and T. Snyder. Baltimore, Md.: Johns Hopkins University Press.

———. 2005. "Mexican Migration to the United States: A Long Twentieth Century of Coyotaje." CCIS Working Paper No. 124. La Jolla: Center for Comparative Immigration Studies, University of California, San Diego, http://www.ccis-ucsd.org/PUBLICATIONS/wrkg124.pdf.

Winograd, Ben. 2004. "Crossing the Border, Again and Again," *Tucson Citizen*, November 5.

2
Profiles of the Research Communities

YESENIA BARAJAS, JAMES BESADA, ELISABETH VALDEZ-SUITER, AND CAITLIN WHITE

Upon arriving in Las Ánimas, Zacatecas, and Tlacuitapa, Jalisco, one notices the many physical characteristics these two migrant-sending towns share: an arid landscape, a dispersed pattern of home settlement, and cattle roaming for miles around. Although the towns are located in different states and are roughly 250 miles apart, they inhabit the same infertile region of Mexico's west-central plateau. Each has only one main road into town. Whereas the ride into Las Ánimas is straight and quickly navigated, the serpentine route to Tlacuitapa takes one through miles of quiet, rolling desert that was the scene of vicious fighting during the Cristero Rebellion of the 1920s. Upon entering the towns, one takes note of the vibrant colors of newly built, often expansive houses scattered among older, simpler homes. The newer, larger dwellings are visible signs of migrants' success in the United States.

But there are also notable contrasts between the two towns. These are apparent even in the towns' plazas. The central plaza of Las Ánimas shows no signs of life, even on a weekend. It is pure concrete; there are no trees, no grass, no benches, and, most of the time, no people. Tlacuitapa's plaza reveals a livelier town. Green lawns, freshly painted benches, and a festive red and yellow gazebo adorn its central plaza. Unlike the plaza in Las Ánimas, the plaza in Tlacuitapa is surrounded by commercial activity: the *Salón Corona* located beyond the southern side of the plaza, the elderly woman who sells pork rinds on the corner, the competing small convenience stores that sell everything from fruit to candles to laundry detergent. Unlike Las Ánimas, where the church and plaza are unconnected, the church in Tlacuitapa stands majestically on the northern side of the plaza and is the focal point of the town.

Tlacuitapeño and Animeño migrants begin trickling back to their hometowns from the United States toward the end of December, but it is not until mid- to late January, when the towns' annual fiestas take place, that the majority have arrived.[1] In the last forty years, the remaining residents of these towns have become accustomed to an absentee population. Many children in Tlacuitapa and Las Ánimas have grown up without their fathers, and the towns are noticeably devoid of young and middle-aged adults—particularly males—for ten months of the year. It is not until the January fiestas, when the migrants return, that the gender and age gaps within the towns are temporarily narrowed.

It is during this time of year that the procession of cars arrives, displaying license plates from assorted U.S. states, mainly California and Oklahoma. In Tlacuitapa, the local priest sprinkled holy water to bless the cars, trucks, and SUVs of the community's *hijos ausentes* (literally "absent sons and daughters") as they drove by the entrance of the church, the vehicles' occupants still weary from the long drive from the United States. The town is filled with vendors selling everything from food to pirated music to artisan goods. The *norteños* bring their children to take their First Communion in the local church. Many marriages are performed as old lovers are reunited. Single young men return looking for brides, while single young women search among the returned young men for potential husbands who have found success in the United States. In the central plaza, U.S.-born children play with each other, laughing and yelling in English. It is the one time of the year when the streets are filled with people, most of whom are quick to tell you that they are not really from there—at least not anymore.

Las Ánimas and Tlacuitapa are representative of many small towns throughout Mexico that have been transformed by migration to the United States. This chapter examines the roots of out-migration from Tlacuitapa and Las Ánimas by exploring the history, economies, and

---

[1] Our research team visited Tlacuitapa during the town's annual fiestas, whereas the annual festivities in Las Ánimas were approaching but had not yet begun when our field interviewing was completed. For this reason, we were able to interview more returned migrants in Tlacuitapa (where 437 people were interviewed) than in Las Ánimas (where we interviewed 166 persons).

demographics of the two towns, as well as government policies that have affected their residents.

TLACUITAPA AND LAS ÁNIMAS: AN INTRODUCTION

Tlacuitapa is in the *municipio* (county) of Unión de San Antonio, one of twenty-six *municipios* in the Los Altos de Jalisco region (Orozco 1992). Although Jalisco is a Pacific coastal state, the Los Altos region (literally, the highlands) lies in the state's northeastern corner and has little to do with the ocean. When political scientist Ann Craig visited the area in the late 1970s to study agrarian reform in the *municipio* of Lagos de Moreno, northeast of Tlacuitapa, she described the Los Altos region as

> characterized by poor soil and highly variable rainfall, an overwhelmingly *mestizo* population, a pattern of small landholdings, devout Catholicism, conservative politics, and an economy based on dairy farming and small-scale cultivation of maize, beans, and chiles (Craig 1983: 12).

These characteristics have persisted to the present day and have been important determinants of out-migration from the region.

Driving about two hours west of Tlacuitapa, one comes to the small town of Las Ánimas, in the *municipio* of Nochistlán de Mejía in Zacatecas State. Like Tlacuitapa, Las Ánimas is located in Mexico's central-west highlands and has the same arid climate and stubborn soil that characterize the entire Los Altos region. In addition to its geographic proximity to Los Altos, Las Ánimas identifies more with that region than with its own state in terms of its economy and culture (Cornelius 1990a: 10). Also like Tlacuitapa, Las Ánimas is somewhat isolated. Its closest neighbor is the county seat of Nochistlán, five kilometers away. The closest major commercial cities, Guadalajara to the south and Aguascalientes to the east, are both two hours away by car.

Despite heavy out-migration to the United States, Tlacuitapa's total population has been rather stable: approximately 1,500 in most censuses conducted since 1950. This population stability was due to replenishment immigration from nearby, smaller localities. The Las Ánimas population peaked in 1979 at about 1,300 and appears to have declined below 1,000 by 2005.

In addition to being smaller than Tlacuitapa, Las Ánimas also has developed at a slower rate in terms of basic urban infrastructure. Elementary schools were established in Tlacuitapa in the 1950s, and a secondary school opened in the 1960s. Infrastructural improvements such as roads, electricity, and potable water had arrived in the community by the 1970s (see table 2.1). In contrast, in 1989 in Las Ánimas there was only one primary school and one *"tele-secundaria"* (distance-learning high school), and the town still lacked potable water, a sewage system, health care facilities, telephone service, a street grid, and a central plaza. The only way of getting to Las Ánimas in 1989 was over a badly deteriorated, unpaved road from Nochistlán, which turned into an impassable mess during the rainy season (Cornelius 1990b: 10).

Table 2.1. Urban Services Improvements in Tlacuitapa

Urban Service	Year Introduced
Bus service to Lagos de Moreno	1942
Postal service	~1942
Elementary school (private)	1956
Elementary school (public)	1958
Secondary school	1967
Electricity	1970
Local road	1974
Clinic	1975
Telephone	1975
Potable water	1976

Both towns have seen infrastructure improvements in recent years, largely funded with migrant earnings generated in the United States. The major infrastructural deficiencies that Cornelius observed in Las Ánimas in 1989 no longer exist; potable water, plumbing, telephone service, and a health clinic were introduced during the 1990s. Animeño migrant organizations, as well as larger regional and statewide clubs, have made significant contributions to urban infrastructure in Las Ánimas since the 1990s. One older resident of Las Ánimas praised the

Club Las Ánimas in Los Angeles for building a water treatment plant, while another Animeño thanked the regional Club Nochistlense for contributing funds to improve the town garden. Another older Animeño, who now lives in San Diego, credited groups of Animeños in California for funding construction of the town's central plaza in 2004, at a cost of US$170,000. In Tlacuitapa, a new bridge, complete with ornate lampposts, had been constructed and the town's church had been expanded, with contributions from *norteños*. Thanks also to migrant remittances, many residents in both Tlacuitapa and Las Ánimas have remodeled their homes in U.S. fashion, and some have built relatively luxurious villa-style houses.

Housing and urban infrastructure in Tlacuitapa and Las Ánimas undoubtedly have improved in recent decades, but these improvements can be misleading. For example, houses might have newly stuccoed facades and neat front yards, but a walk around to the rear often reveals that they sit on foundations of deteriorated brick. Some families have become relatively well-off working abroad and have invested substantial amounts in their homes and hometowns. However, these improvements are not spread evenly among the population. Moreover, many construction projects are left unfinished because there is no one to finish the work, most of the town's able-bodied residents having migrated to the United States. Leaving the towns' centers, the paved roads soon give way to dirt roads, street signs end, and the chatter of residents' conversation turns into the barnyard sounds of cows, horses, chickens, and donkeys—reminders that, despite recent improvements, these are still humble agricultural communities.

Colonial Remnants: Lasting Influences of the Spanish Crown and Church

The characteristics of present-day Tlacuitapa and Las Ánimas have been shaped by the unique history of the Los Altos region. When Spanish conquistadores arrived in Los Altos, the region was controlled by Chichimeca Indians. In combination, the region's harsh climate and the nomadic lifestyle of the Chichimecas help explain why there was never an indigenous population stable enough to leave deep cultural roots in this region, whose later ethnic makeup has been predominantly mestizo.

The Spanish conquistadores entered the area via Teúl and No-
chistlán and won a key victory over the Chichimecas in September 1541
(Fábregas 1979). This victory was a turning point in the region's history.
Though the Spaniards' political influence was short lived, their cultural
and religious influences remained strong. The area's mainly mestizo
population revered both the Catholic Church and the Spanish Crown.
Hence, when Mexico fought for independence in the early 1800s, the
Spaniards had little difficulty appealing to regional pride to encourage
Alteños to see themselves as loyal servants of God and the Spanish
Crown (as they still do today), rather than as part of the newly emerg-
ing independent nation (Fábregas 1979).

The area's strong religious fervor has manifested itself in migration.
When confronting the challenge of an undocumented border crossing
into the United States, migrants pray to Santo Toribio Romo González,
who is said to have performed miracles to help undocumented migrants cross the border.[2] Santo Toribio's shrine attracts between 250,000
and 300,000 visitors per year (Borden 2003). Thousands of migrants and
their families have made the pilgrimage to the shrine to ask for protec-
tion or to give thanks for a safe return. Among the offerings they have
left are notes of thanks, dollar bills, a sonogram, and drawings of Santo
Toribio and people jumping the fence into the United States. Santo
Toribio and his shrine represent the Church-sanctioned support of
migration in this region, demonstrating the extent to which undocumented migration to the United States has been embedded in the local
religious culture.

The Shaping of Two Agricultural Economies

The Spaniards' mestizo descendants, much like the region's residents
today, based their economy largely on agriculture, livestock raising,
and dairy farming. Given the focus on agriculture, the land tenure systems prevailing in Tlacuitapa and Las Ánimas had significant impacts

---

[2] Santo Toribio, the patron saint of migrants, was murdered by a group of sol-
diers and *agraristas* during the Cristero Rebellion in 1928 and canonized by the
Catholic Church in 2000, along with twenty-six other martyrs of the Cristero
wars (Diocesan Migrant and Refugee Services, Inc. n.d.).

on the economy of each community. Tlacuitapa received an *ejido* land grant in the 1930s when the Mexican government redistributed large landholdings to peasant communities. Tlacuitapa's first *ejido* was created in 1937, with land parcels distributed to 206 individuals. By the mid-1990s there were 170 *ejidatarios* in the community, still sufficient to make Tlacuitapa's *ejido* the largest among the eighteen *ejidos* in the *municipio* of Unión de San Antonio (Cornelius 1998: 235).

In 1992, Article 27 of the Mexican Constitution was amended to allow the privatization of *ejido* land,[3] sparking concern that large numbers of *ejidatarios* would sell their land and migrate to find work in the United States. However, a 1995 study in Tlacuitapa found that the constitutional reform had virtually no impact on Tlacuitapeños' propensity to migrate. In fact, *ejidatarios*, who tended to be older and preferred to stay at home, were less likely to migrate than were private landholders and landless workers (Cornelius 1998: 239). Though *ejidatarios* interviewed in Tlacuitapa in 1995 expressed a desire for their children to remain in the community and carry on the agricultural tradition, an overwhelming number of *ejidatarios* and other Tlacuitapeño residents (83.9 and 80.5 percent, respectively) acknowledged that migration was necessary if a young person was to "get ahead" in life (Cornelius 1998: 241). Since the 1970s, the children of *ejidatarios* have been among the most migration-prone groups in the community (Cornelius 1979: 17). As the population grows and the amount of available *ejido* land remains constant or decreases, the children of *ejidatarios* must search elsewhere for income.

Unlike Tlacuitapa, Las Ánimas never received a grant of *ejido* land. Agricultural economist Richard Mines, who spent two years studying Las Ánimas in the late 1970s, concluded that the enormous Casteñada hacienda near Las Ánimas had profound and lasting effects on the town, contravening an *ejido* system, creating new social classes, and even determining who would migrate to the United States (Mines 1981: chap. 5). In the early 1900s the Castañedas controlled the bulk of land in Las Ánimas and employed the majority of the townspeople as share-

---

[3] Formerly, *ejidatarios* had use rights to the land but could not legally sell it or rent it out—though many did so nevertheless, illegally.

croppers, day laborers, or shepherds on the hacienda. The small "middle sector" of hacienda managers and foremen (about thirty families) were the first to migrate to the United States because they were the only families who could afford to do so. Beginning in the 1920s, these families established themselves in the United States as legal residents, while also investing money in land purchases and housing construction in Las Ánimas. However, because these families were based in the United States, the land they purchased in Mexico was not worked but served only as a symbol of a family's wealth. Mines notes this paradox:

> There is shortage of labor for those who have land, and a shortage of land for those who have willing labor. Those with the land and income to improve it do not hold land for income. Those interested in improving the land for income, in general, do not own it or have the semi-skilled California job needed to finance improvements. Both groups, having better California-side than village-side options, avoid work in their home town (1981: 113).

Previous studies of these towns identified the lack of adequate irrigation and water access as barriers to agricultural production. In 1990 Cornelius noted that "virtually all agriculture in Las Ánimas is rainfall-dependent and uses only the most traditional, unmechanized technologies."[4] Corn was the main crop in both communities in 1990, but "virtually all of it is self-consumed or used as cattle feed," and most arable land was used for pasture (Cornelius 1990b: 283). Despite these obstacles, farming has long been the most prominent economic activity for Tlacuitapeños and Animeños. In 1976, 25 percent of individuals interviewed in Tlacuitapa worked in agriculture (Cornelius 1976). And among our 2005 interviewees who stated they had worked in their hometowns during the previous year, agricultural work was still the most common type of employment in both towns, employing 18 per-

---

[4] The unmechanized technologies Cornelius observed in 1990 were actually an improvement over what Mines found in the 1970s in Las Ánimas, when farmers employed young boys to till the land. As increasing out-migration created a labor shortage, they switched to plow animals for tilling (Mines 1981: 126–27).

cent of Tlacuitapeños and 43 percent of Animeños. Interviewees from Las Ánimas were more likely to own their land and to cultivate it, even though irrigation seems more accessible in Tlacuitapa (see table 2.2). The predominant crop in both communities in 2005 was corn, as has been the case throughout the towns' recent agricultural histories.

Table 2.2. Land Use in Tlacuitapa and Las Ánimas, 2005

	Tlacuitapa (N = 408)	Las Ánimas (N = 154)
Percentage of interviewees who own land	19.90%	35.70%
Of landholders, average number of hectares in their possession	17.55	10.14
Of landholders, median number of hectares in their possession	6.5	4.75
Of landholders, range of hectares in their possession	0.25 to 120	0.5 to 80
Percentage of landholders who own cultivated land	69.90%	94.10%
Of people with cultivated land, average number of hectares cultivated	6.37	4.9
Of people with cultivated land, median number of hectares cultivated	4	3
Of people with cultivated land, range of hectares cultivated	1 to 50	0.5 to 17
Percentage of landholders who own irrigated land	37.10%	25%
Of people with irrigated land, average number of hectares irrigated	6.29	2.75
Of people with irrigated land, median number of hectares irrigated	4	1.5
Of people with irrigated land, range of hectares irrigated	1 to 50	1 to 7
Percentage of landholders who…		
grow corn	69.60%	92.70%
grow beans	7.60%	34.50%
grow alfalfa	5.10%	5.50%
grow vegetables	0%	1.80%
grow sorghum	0%	1.80%
grow other crop	3.80%	10.90%

Although significant numbers of people in these towns are still culti-vating land and growing crops, cattle raising has been the most viable agricultural activity for individuals in Tlacuitapa. Alarcón reports that cattle raising was originally pursued to provide meat and milk for fam-ily consumption. When Nestlé established a milk-processing plant in nearby Lagos de Moreno in 1943, however, the Los Altos region con-centrated on dairy farming and became the leader in milk production in Jalisco (Alarcón 1989: 9). According to Guadalupe Rodríguez Gómez (2000: 37), the Los Altos region accounted for 85 percent of milk pro-duction in Jalisco and 13 percent of milk production nationwide by the end of the 1990s. Given the area's semi-arid climate and poor soils, which cannot guarantee consistent crop production, most dairy farmers rely entirely on commercial cattle feed, raising production costs and placing farmers at the mercy of a fluctuating feed market. Farmers also face domestic price controls on the milk sold to consumers. These types of restraints have led to low productivity levels. Rodríguez Gómez explains the challenges facing the average small Los Altos dairy farmer:

> First, regional milk production is highly fragmented and geographically dispersed. Second, dairy farms usually function as small-scale, family-based units of production. Third, producers make minimal capital investments; they have very limited access to institu-tional credit, and there is no regional tradition of in-vesting in dairy farming. Fourth, the region's cattle— generally "pinto" or "criollo" varieties, a poor quality Holstein mix—are well adapted to the terrain but are poor milk producers. And fifth, over 70 percent of small farms and 20 percent of midsize farms in Los Al-tos have little or no mechanization; only the largest farms are highly mechanized and stocked with good cattle (Rodríguez Gómez 2000: 37).

Although the milk industry has been a primary source of income for many small farmers in the region for years, the constraints outlined above make it unlikely that they will be able to continue to be profitable far into the future. As agricultural production remains hindered by climate and dairy farming becomes less lucrative, farmers will continue to search for new, more stable means of sustenance.

DEMOGRAPHY

Though the populations of Tlacuitapa and Las Ánimas share similarities, they also display some noteworthy differences. The Las Ánimas population we surveyed in 2005 was older on average: the median age was 44 years, and 44 percent of our interviewees were over 45 years of age. In contrast, the median age in Tlacuitapa was 30, with only 26 percent falling in the 46–65 age range. Thirty-eight percent of people interviewed in Tlacuitapa were between the ages of 15 and 25, while only 19 percent of Animeños were in this age range. Since Animeños tended to be older, they also were more likely to be married and to have children: 61 percent of Animeños were married and had children, compared to 52 percent of Tlacuitapeños.

The majority of people we interviewed had worked during the past year, and most of these had worked in their hometown rather than in the United States (53 percent in Tlacuitapa; 65 percent in Las Ánimas). As noted above, among the interviewees who stated they had worked in their hometowns during the past year, agriculture was the most common activity in both towns. In Tlacuitapa, the second most common job was dairy work (9.4 percent) and the third most common occupation was construction worker/peon (8.9 percent). In Las Ánimas, the second most common occupation was sharecropper (14 percent), and seamstress and *albañil* tied for third place, at 6 percent each. Of the 21.5 percent who did *not* work in their hometowns the year prior to the time of the interview, 80 percent were women. It is not surprising, then, that the majority of nonworking interviewees who resided in Tlacuitapa and Las Ánimas in the year prior to our survey identified themselves as housewives.

MIGRATION TO "EL NORTE"

Although Tlacuitapa and Las Ánimas are both agrarian-based communities, agriculture no longer generates sufficient income to sustain most

of the towns' families. Sending migrants to the United States has become the most viable way of survival and economic advancement in
both communities. Migration to the United States has been occurring
for nearly a century. The first migration wave began in the early 1900s
(sparked by the Mexican Revolution), peaked in the 1920s, and died off
by the 1930s, when the Great Depression wiped out the United States'
demand for workers. During this first wave, migrants found employment in U.S. agriculture, railroad construction, factories, and mining.
For example, pioneering migrants from Las Ánimas worked in the
Bethlehem Metal Foundry in San Francisco, and by 1980 South San
Francisco was reported to host the "oldest and most concentrated
community" of Animeños in the United States (Mines 1981: 23).

   The second wave of migration from both communities occurred
between 1942 and 1964, when four million Mexicans—principally experienced farmworkers—came to the United States to work in agriculture under the bracero contract labor program. Both men and women
from Tlacuitapa and Las Ánimas worked as braceros in the 1950s and
1960s, typically laboring for six months at a time in seasonal agricultural work in California, Texas, Oregon, and the Southwest. Antonio,
an ex-bracero now living in Tlacuitapa, described the conditions in
which the braceros lived:

> They housed us in barracks. There were some sixty peo-
> ple in each barrack. People would joke every time new
> detainees arrived. They'd say, "Now we really aren't go-
> ing to fit," and the Border Patrol would say, "How could
> you not fit?"

   When these work contracts expired with the end of the bracero
program in 1964, braceros were required to hand in their work permits
and return to Mexico. However, some braceros obtained legal status
with help from their U.S. employers and stayed in the United States,
working in various nonagricultural occupations, such as construction,
hotels, and restaurants. In this sense, the bracero program opened some
doors to nonagricultural employment for Mexicans in the United States.
But its termination also unleashed a new wave of undocumented Mexican migration. As Mines notes, some Animeños began working as un-

documented migrants even before the bracero program ended because they were paid better salaries in the United States and could work more hours there than they could in Mexico. Undocumented migration from Las Ánimas to the United States during the final years of the bracero program was also driven by a severe drought that forced agricultural workers to find alternate sources of income (Mines 1981: 83).

The third significant wave of migration from our research communities began in the mid-1960s, following the end of the bracero program (see figure 2.1). Mines argues that two "fundamental shifts" accompanied this new phase of undocumented migration to the United States and molded migratory patterns into what they are today. The first shift was increasing migration to U.S. cities, as opposed to the traditional rural receiving areas, with a corresponding increase in employment in construction, factories, and services, as opposed to agriculture. For example, many Animeños came to California to work for a construction cleanup company headed by an Animeño, which operates in Los Angeles, San Bernardino, and Orange counties. The second change at the end of the bracero program was a shift toward legal status, with legal residents jumping from 16.1 percent of total Animeño migrants in 1959 to 37.1 percent in 1962. Their new legal status prompted more migrants to settle permanently, establishing important satellite communities that help first-time migrants find housing and employment in the United States. As Mines explains, "Once settler colonies were established, a huge wave of Animeños flooded into California.... By 1968 the U.S. city population definitively surpassed the U.S. town population," and by 1974, "59.6 percent of all adult male Animeños worked in California" (Mines 1981: 88).

The combination of various Mexican economic crises (in 1982, 1986, and 1993) and the U.S. legalization programs of the late 1980s (created by the Immigration Reform and Control Act of 1986) sparked a new era of emigration from Tlacuitapa and Las Ánimas in the 1980s and 1990s (see figure 2.1). Numerous Tlacuitapeño male family heads took advantage of IRCA's legalization program for undocumented farmworkers to begin the process of obtaining "green cards" (permanent U.S. resident visas). An important feature of Animeño migration in the 1980s which Goldring (1990) observed is that, although workers settled in various

Figure 2.1. U.S.-Bound Migration (first trip, legal and undocumented) from Tlacuitapa and Las Ánimas, 1948–2002

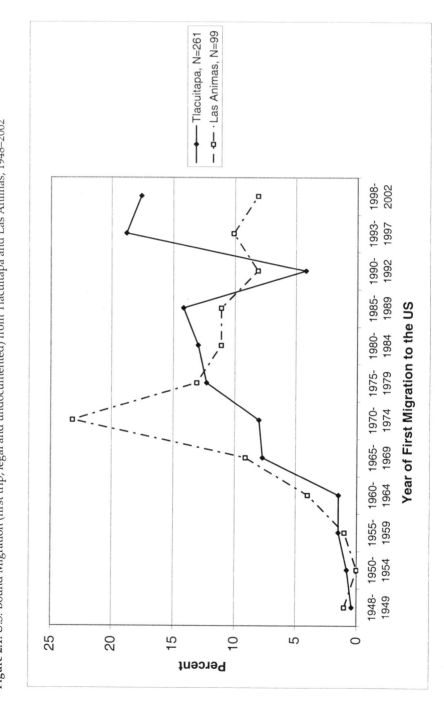

localities throughout California, they nevertheless remained a tight-knit community due to continuous communication between satellite communities and frequent reunions and events (such as the biannual baseball games). This connection between Animeños, despite the geographic distances that separated them, is particularly strong, and we see its value today in the community projects that Animeño migrant groups in California have funded in their hometown, such as the central plaza.

References

Alarcón, Rafael. 1989. "Gracias a Dios y al Norte: Tlacuitapa, Jalisco, y su relación con los Estados Unidos." Unpublished paper. La Jolla: Center for U.S.-Mexican Studies, University of California, San Diego.

Borden, Tessie. 2003. "Border Saints," *Hispanic Magazine*, April, http://www.elpasodiocese.org/DMRS/SanTori/BorderSaints.htm, accessed June 2005.

Cornelius, Wayne A. 1976. "Outmigration from Rural Mexican Communities." In *The Dynamics of Migration: International Migration*. Occasional Monographs Series, No. 5, Vol. 2. Washington, D.C.: Interdisciplinary Communications Program, Smithsonian Institution.

———. 1979. "Policy Impacts on Rural Out-Migration: The Case of Los Altos de Jalisco." In *Población y desarrollo en el oeste de México*, ed. William Winnie and Jesús Arroyo. Guadalajara, Jal.: Facultad de Economía, Universidad de Guadalajara.

———. 1990a. "Labor Migration to the United States: Development Outcomes and Alternatives in Mexican Sending Communities." Final Report to the Commission for the Study of International Migration and Cooperative Economic Development, Washington D.C., March.

———. 1990b. "Impacts of the 1986 U.S. Immigration Law on Emigration from Rural Mexican Sending Communities." In *Undocumented Migration to the United States: IRCA and the Experience of the 1980s*, ed. Frank D. Bean et al. Santa Monica, Calif. and Washington, D.C.: RAND Corporation/Urban Institute.

———. 1998. "Ejido Reform: Stimulus or Alternative to Migration?" In *The Transformation of Rural Mexico: Reforming the Ejido Sector*, edited by Wayne A. Cornelius and David Myhre. La Jolla: Center for U.S.-Mexican Studies, University of California, San Diego.

Craig, Ann L. 1983. *The First Agraristas: An Oral History of a Mexican Agrarian Reform Movement.* Berkeley: University of California Press.

Diocesan Migrant and Refugee Services, Inc. n.d. "Santo Toribio Romo González: Patron of Migrants and Border Crossers, Patrón de los migrantes," http://www.elpasodiocese.org/DMRS/SanTori/Infopage.htm.

Fábregas, Andrés. 1979. "Los Altos de Jalisco: características generales." In *El movimiento cristero: sociedad y conflicto en Los Altos de Jalisco,* ed. José Díaz and Román Rodríguez. México, D.F.: Centro de Investigaciones Superiores del Instituto Nacional de Antropología e Historia.

Goldring, Luin. 1990. "Development and Migration: A Comparative Study of Two Mexican Migrant Circuits." Working Paper No. 37. Washington, D.C.: Commission for the Study of International Migration and Cooperative Economic Development.

Mines, Richard. 1981. *Developing a Community Tradition of Migration to the United States: A Field Study in Rural Zacatecas, Mexico, and California Settlement Areas.* La Jolla: Center for U.S.-Mexican Studies, University of California, San Diego.

Orozco, Juan Luis. 1992. *El negocio de los ilegales: ¿ganancias para quién?* Guadalajara, Jal.: Editorial Agata/ITESO.

Rodríguez Gómez, Guadalupe. 2000. "A Matter of Quality: Power and Change among Dairy Farmers in Los Altos de Jalisco." In *Strategies for Resource Management, Production, and Marketing in Rural Mexico,* ed. Guadalupe Rodríguez Gómez and Richard Snyder. La Jolla: Center for U.S.-Mexican Studies, University of California, San Diego.

3

The Contemporary Migration Process

SEIDY GAYTÁN, EVELYN LUCIO, FAWAD SHAIQ, AND
ANJANETTE URDANIVIA

> *I have a message for all who judge us in America: it is hor-
> rible to be separated from your family, with some in Mexico
> and others in the United States. There are fathers who have
> never met their children and children who have never met
> or don't remember their fathers. And when they come home
> to visit, they feel like strangers in their own homes. It's a
> cold, disheartening feeling.*—Tania, a 21-year-old un-
> documented migrant from Tlacuitapa whose father and
> brother migrated to the United States in 1990.

> *I am more afraid of what will happen to me if I stay in Mex-
> ico than if I go to the United States.*—Pedro, a 32-year-old
> undocumented migrant from Las Ánimas.

Migration to the United States has a long and deep tradition in Tlacuitapa and Las Ánimas. Chapter 2's broad overview of our research communities allows us to place this migration in context. Against that
background, this chapter takes a closer look at the characteristics and
motivations of those who have migrated and those who opted to remain in their hometown. We begin by comparing the demographic and
occupational profiles of experienced migrants and nonmigrants. We
then provide a detailed analysis of reasons for migrating and for *not*
migrating, including the micro- and macro-economic factors that influence decisions to go north and the transnational social networks that
facilitate migration to the United States.

DEMOGRAPHIC AND OCCUPATIONAL PROFILES
Experienced Migrants

U.S.-bound migration is widespread among residents of Tlacuitapa and Las Ánimas, with 64 percent of our interviewees having migrated to the United States at least once and over half planning to migrate in 2005.[1] Table 3.1 summarizes the demographic characteristics of experienced migrants. Although more women have migrated in recent decades than was true in the past, men remain much more likely to make the journey across the border. Three-fourths of all men interviewed in our 2005 survey reported having migrated to the United States at least once, contrasted with approximately one-fourth of the women interviewed.

Table 3.1. Demographic Characteristics of Experienced Migrants

Average age	35.7 years
Percent of men with migration experience	75.8%
Percent of women with migration experience	26.7%
Percent married	73.4%
Average number of children	2.7
Average years of education	5.6

N = 354.

Although nearly three-fourths of experienced migrants in our survey were married, less than 40 percent of the married men reported taking their spouses with them to the United States on their most recent sojourn. It is more common for married men to migrate alone, sending money to their wives and children who remain in the home community. Many single men migrate as well, sending remittances to their parents, siblings, and extended family members. However, single men do not face the same economic pressures as married men, for whom

[1] According to a recent study by Parametría (2005), which conducts research and public opinion polls on topics related to Mexico and Latin America, 23 percent of the general Mexican population was considering migrating to the United States for work in 2005. This statistic is markedly lower than the share of Tlacuitapeños and Animeños who told us they planned to migrate in 2005. Yet, given that Jalisco and Zacatecas are two of the most important migrant-sending states in Mexico, our finding is in line with expectations.

migration is more of a financial necessity, especially for married men with children (experienced migrants had 2.7 children on average). Florentino, a 54-year-old resident of Las Ánimas, explained, "I didn't think about going to the United States when I was young or when I was a teenager. I didn't find it appealing. It was not until I got married that I decided to go because of economic necessity."

There is a major difference between the experienced migrants interviewed in 2005 and those surveyed by Wayne Cornelius in 1989 with respect to educational attainment (Cornelius 1990). Total years of schooling among experienced migrants averaged 4.24 in the 1989 survey, substantially lower than the 5.6-year average reported in 2005 (see table 3.1). One key explanation for this difference is that the secondary school in Tlacuitapa, the town where we conducted the bulk of our interviews, is only a few years old. Previously, Tlacuitapeño children who wanted to continue their education past primary school had to commute to Lagos de Moreno, about 30 miles away. The expense of the commute meant that fewer children continued their education.

The overwhelming majority of experienced migrants interviewed in 2005 travel to the same regions in the United States and work there in a handful of industries. On their most recent trip to the United States, half of the experienced migrants worked in California, with the majority living in and around the San Francisco Bay Area. One large community of migrants has been established in Union City, 20 miles south of Oakland. Following California was Oklahoma, with 21.9 percent of experienced migrants; nearly all migrants to Oklahoma live in Oklahoma City. Antonio Muñoz, who was born and raised in Tlacuitapa, migrated to Oklahoma City at 16 years of age and has since established one of Oklahoma's largest bridge construction firms. His company, which in 2005 employed twenty-four migrants from Tlacuitapa, was the principal magnet drawing Tlacuitapeños to Oklahoma City, beginning in the 1980s. Small but significant clusters of migrants also reside and work in Chicago, Las Vegas, Dallas, and Detroit, and others are dispersed throughout the United States.

Migrants begin to work almost immediately after arriving in the United States. The U.S. occupations of experienced migrants from our 2005 sample and from Cornelius's 1989 survey are reported in table 3.2.

In both surveys, the most common job for migrants on their last trip to the United States was construction, followed by work in the service sector, which includes restaurants, janitorial work, gardening, and caregiving for children and the elderly. Interestingly, only 10 percent of migrants interviewed in 2005 worked in agriculture, where employment tends to be seasonal. Even in 1989, the percentage of migrants employed in agricultural work was not high. This suggests that the large majority of migrants have permanent, year-round jobs, contradicting the common notion that migrants only come to the United States for seasonal employment. We found a significant increase in employment in the construction industry since 1989, which undoubtedly reflects the success of Antonio Muñoz's company in Oklahoma, which has led to the employment of Tlacuitapa migrants not only in his company but also in other construction firms in Oklahoma City. The share of migrants employed in manufacturing has decreased since 1989, which may reflect the relocation of some U.S. manufacturing plants to developing countries, including Mexico, that offer cheaper labor.

Table 3.2. Sectors of U.S. Employment for Experienced Migrants

Employment Sector	1989 Survey	2005 Survey
Construction	26.8%	45.8%
Service sector	20.1%	24.8%
Agriculture	18.1%	10.7%
Manufacturing	17.6%	6.2%
Unemployed	Unavailable	0.6%
Other	17.4%	11.9%
Total	100.0%	100.0%

N = 344.

Nonmigrants

More than a third (36 percent) of our 2005 interviewees had never migrated to the United States; their demographic characteristics appear in table 3.3. Nonmigrants are younger and less likely to be married than are experienced migrants, and they have fewer children to support. Nonmigrants are also more likely to be female; nearly three-fourths of the women interviewed had never migrated.[2] Nonmigrants have more years of education than do experienced migrants, suggesting that some young people in these communities may be pursuing higher education rather than migrating to the United States.

Table 3.3. Demographic Characteristics of Nonmigrants, 2005

Average age	31.5 years
Percent of men with no migration experience	24.2%
Percent of women with no migration experience	73.3%
Percent married	25.7%
Average number of children	1.1
Average years of education	6.6

N = 210.

As shown in table 3.4, nonmigrants in Tlacuitapa and Las Ánimas have a more diversified occupational profile than experienced migrants, with almost equal shares in agriculture, services, and construction. It is interesting that the agricultural sector is so well represented among nonmigrants, given that most townspeople complain that falling prices for agricultural products and rising prices for agricultural inputs have undercut the sector's profitability.

Table 3.4. Sectors of Employment for Nonmigrants

Agriculture	27.4%
Services	21.5%
Construction	20.0%
Manufacturing	7.9%
Other	20.0%
Unemployed	3.2%
Total	100.0%

N = 178.

The fact that many people continue in agriculture suggests that there are few other alternatives. What little construction work is available tends to involve building "vacation homes" for migrants who

---

[2] Gender differences with respect to migration are discussed in more detail in chapter 6.

invest their U.S. earnings in residences in the home community. Most of these houses are empty for the better part of the year and are only used when the migrants return for visits. Such construction work is not a stable, sustainable source of employment, since the rate at which these homes are built will taper off. Nonmigrants surveyed in 2005 were more likely than migrants to be unemployed. Given that the majority of migrants go to the United States for economic reasons (to be discussed below), it is not unreasonable to assume that many nonmigrants will soon join the ranks of those going north.

SHOULD I STAY OR SHOULD I GO?

Why Some Remain

Numerous factors motivate people in Tlacuitapa and Las Ánimas to migrate to the United States. Yet a significant fraction of the population opts to remain at home. Examining the reasons why people decide to migrate or not to migrate allows us to understand the pros and cons involved in the migration decision. We asked people with no migration experience whether they were planning to migrate in 2005. For those who replied in the negative, we asked, "Why do you not want to go north [to the United States] this year?" The most common reason for not migrating was a lack of economic need, followed by apprehension over clandestine border crossings (see table 3.5).

Table 3.5. Reasons Given by Nonmigrants for Not Migrating in 2005

No economic need	18.7%
Difficult to cross border without papers	14.4%
Not interested in migrating	13.7%
Too old or too young	13.0%
Family difficulties	11.5%
Can't pay for *coyote* and transportation	7.2%
Other	21.5%
Total	100.0%

N = 139.

In his studies of migration from southern Mexico to the United States, Jeffrey Cohen argues that lack of access to social networks is a leading reason why potential migrants do not migrate. Marco Martínez, a nonmigrant from Oaxaca who was interviewed for Cohen's study, explained why he has been unable to migrate:

> How can we afford to migrate? I have my children to feed; I have my wife and my mother-in-law. I can't leave them alone. Even if I did, where would I get the money to get across the border? Who would help me? Where would I live? I can't do it. I don't even think about it (Cohen 2004: 131).

But unlike Marco, the overwhelming majority of Tlacuitapa and Las Ánimas residents surveyed in 2005 said they did have family living in the United States. It would appear, therefore, that the nonmigrants in our survey town are not kept from migrating by the lack of a social network in the United States. It may be, however, that migrants and nonmigrants have different kinds of ties with relatives in the United States, with experienced migrants having closer (nuclear) family in the United States and nonmigrants having only more distant relatives there, which would make their migration relatively more difficult.

Motives for Migration

Economic Drivers

The majority of experienced migrants in the 2005 survey cited economic reasons as their principal motivation for going to the United States (see table 3.6). This finding is consistent with most studies of Mexican out-migration. According to Richard Mines, who studied migrants from Las Ánimas in 1981:

> The principal motivation for out-migration, temporary or permanent, of Mexico's poor to the United States is a search for economic security. The decision makers in each family unit perceive that working with local resources cannot provide an adequate standard of comfort and se-curity.... Individual motivation becomes less important since all men are expected to go to the United States if their families cannot earn a living locally (Mines 1981: 36).

Inequality with regard to income and employment opportunities between sending and receiving countries is consistently identified as one of the fundamental causes of migration flows worldwide, and the cases of Tlacuitapa and Las Ánimas are no exception.

Table 3.6. Motives for Migration

Reasons for Going	On Most Recent Trip[a]	Planning to Migrate in 2005[b]
Economic necessity	34.7%	30.4%
Returning to same job in the U.S.	22.1%	13.9%
Better pay in the United States	8.3%	13.9%
More job opportunities in the U.S.	6.0%	9.6%
No jobs available in Mexico	5.2%	4.3%
All of the above: general economic rationale	76.3%	72.1%
Family reunification	9.5%	12.2%
Other	14.2%	15.7%
Total	100.0%	100.0%

[a] N = 349. [b] N = 115.

As indicated by the response data in table 3.6, migrants are motivated not only by the belief that they can find work more easily in the United States, but also by the expectation that they can find higher-paying jobs than are available in Mexico. Fourteen percent of experienced migrants who were planning to migrate in 2005 cited better pay in the United States as their principal reason for leaving their home community. They echoed the words of one man interviewed in Adam Sherry's 2004 study of unauthorized Mexican migrants attempting to enter the United States through the San Diego/Tijuana corridor:

> I am going [to the United States] to earn more. Why would I stay and work for $10.00 a day when I could get $15.00 an hour in the United States? I mean in Mexico people would be happy to be paid $6.75 an hour to work at McDonalds, but Americans, they won't even think about it. Most people think it is below them. They consider it work for Mexicans.

For many migrants, the monetary costs of migration, the dangers of a clandestine border crossing, and the discomfort of being immersed in a foreign culture were all subordinate to the draw of a greater earning potential in the United States (Sherry 2004: 47). Given that the wage differential between minimum-wage jobs in the United States and in Mexico is often more than eleven to one, it is not surprising that many migrants are opting for employment in the United States.

In fact, many migrants currently look to the United States as their only option for economic success, given their low earnings potential in Mexico. In our survey, nearly three-fourths (71.8 percent) of respondents said that one had to leave their hometown in order to succeed. This finding is consistent with the results of a recent nationwide survey conducted in Mexico by Parametría (2005), which asked: "If you were to go and work in the United States, do you believe that it would resolve your economic problems?" Sixty percent of the general population replied in the affirmative, as did 88 percent of those who were already seriously considering migrating (see figure 3.1).

Family and Social Networks
Although family reunification might not be the primary reason that experienced migrants give for migrating (see table 3.6), family ties facilitate migration by lowering the emotional and economic costs of making the transition to life in the United States. Our findings indicate that 87.4 percent of experienced migrants had family living in the United States prior to their first migration; the median number of family members living in the United States was twenty.

Social networks play a large part in determining a migrant's destination in the United States. Mines argues that "the economic and social environment of an individual or family is defined more by the location of trusted friends and relatives than by geography" (Mines 1981: 35). According to our survey data, 80.1 percent of experienced migrants chose their most recent U.S. destination based on the location of their family and friends. José, a 36-year-old experienced migrant from Las Ánimas, said: "The two times I have migrated to the United States, I went straight to Los Angeles.... It's the only city I know. I have a lot of family residing with me in Los Angeles, and this made it easy for me to

Figure 3.1. Migration as a Solution to Economic Problems

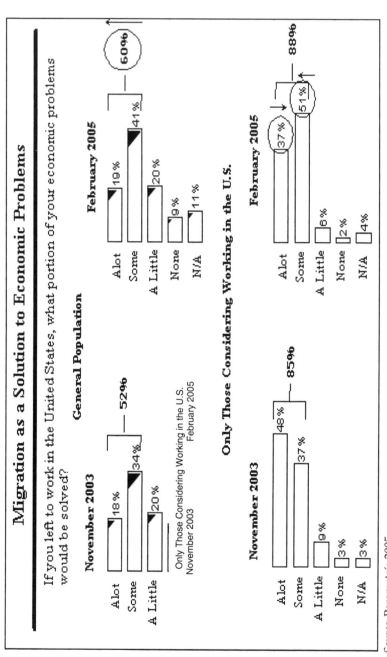

Migration as a Solution to Economic Problems

If you left to work in the United States, what portion of your economic problems would be solved?

General Population

November 2003

Alot — 18%
Some — 34% ⎤ 52%
A Little — 20%

Only Those Considering Working in the U.S.
November 2003

February 2005

Alot — 19%
Some — 41% ⎤ 60%
A Little — 20%
None — 9%
N/A — 11%

Only Those Considering Working in the U.S.
February 2005

Only Those Considering Working in the U.S.

November 2003

Alot — 48% ⎤ 85%
Some — 37%
A Little — 9%
None — 3%
N/A — 3%

February 2005

Alot — 37%
Some — 51% ⎤ 88%
A Little — 6%
None — 2%
N/A — 4%

Source: Parametría 2005.

migrate." Social networks help recent migrants adjust to their new life in the United States emotionally by providing an environment that is reminiscent of home through culture, language, music, and religion. Nazario, a Tlacuitapeño native in his late 50s, recalled what other migrants have relayed to him about life in the United States: "Even though I have never migrated, I have heard that migrants are happy and encounter people from their country in the United States who are willing to talk to them in Spanish or to have a taco."

Perhaps the networks' key usefulness to new migrants is the help they provide in obtaining employment for the newcomers. Communities that count successful pioneers among their migrant members have the best potential to develop migration networks, because the returning pioneer can help relatives cross the border and find work (Mines 1981: 37). In our 2005 sample, 86.2 percent of experienced migrants claimed that finding a job in the United States without papers can be difficult, but fewer than 2 percent felt that it was impossible. The migrants' relative optimism about job-seeking in the United States is grounded in their access to social networks. Cornelius's 1989 study of Tlacuitapa and Las Ánimas found that 45.1 percent of respondents obtained employment in the United States through social network contacts. In our 2005 survey this proportion was 78.1 percent. Jaime, a 21-year-old male from Tlacuitapa who recently migrated to the United States, responded: "You ask how I got my job.... My cousin's aunt got us a job at the restaurant. I live with her, and we both work in the same restaurant." Concepción, a 38-year-old experienced migrant from Tlacuitapa who worked in California, said of her job search, "It was not difficult to find a job. My sister helped me. She recommended me to her supervisor. But without her help, I think it would have been difficult to find a job."

MODELING THE DECISION TO MIGRATE

Logistic regressions were run to determine the relative importance of various factors in the decision to migrate. The first regression, whose results are summarized in table 3.7, examined the relative importance of various factors in the decision to migrate in the previous two years. The regression indicates that the only factor that has contributed to the decision to migrate in the previous two years is the number of times that the respondent had migrated previously. This is contrary to much of the analysis in the migration literature, which argues that age, marital status, education, sector of employment, and number of dependents all contribute to the decision to migrate. There are many possible explanations for this departure from the literature. First, it is likely that many respondents who reported multiple migrations to the United States had extensive social networks that enabled them to migrate back and forth without regard for the other factors that could contribute to the propensity to migrate. This explanation is reinforced by the fact that there was not a statistically significant difference in the number of migrants who had legal documentation that permitted them to migrate to the United States and those who were without authorization. Second, the increased level of border enforcement and the robust U.S. economy at the time of our survey could have introduced sample-selection biases. If many of the recent migrants remained longer in the United States and were therefore not available to be interviewed in their hometowns, then the determinants for the propensity to migrate would be biased estimates.

Table 3.7. Determinants of Migration in 2003, 2004

Characteristics of Post-2003 Border Crossers	β	Standard Error	Significance
Male	−.250	.555	.652
Age	−.034	.078	.665
Age^2	−.000	.001	.961
Married	−.087	.492	.860
Years of education	.086	.094	.360
Dependents	−.124	.140	.374
Worked in agriculture	−.370	.530	.485
Worked in construction	.434	.452	.337
Sense of relative deprivation on scale of 1–10	−.103	.065	.114
Number of migrations	**.193***	.039	.000

The reference category is "no."
Statistically significant at the 90% (* $p < .10$) confidence level.
N = 392.

More enlightening is our analysis of the intent to migrate in 2005. Table 3.8 reports the results from a logit model regression of all experienced migrants who were asked if they planned to migrate again in the coming year. Educational attainment, marital status, and the number of dependents were not strong indicators for the intent to migrate. This is again contrary to some of the results in the literature that would argue that (1) higher educational levels provide more economic opportunities in Mexico, (2) married persons are less likely to migrate, and (3) persons with more dependents are less likely to migrate. However, there were other factors that characterized the respondents that reported their intent to migrate.

Table 3.8. Determinants of Intent to Migrate in 2005

Characteristics of Migrants Saying "Yes," Plan to Migrate in 2005[a]	β	Standard Error	Significance
Male	.748 **	.314	.017
Age	.110 **	.053	.039
Age^2	−.002 **	.001	.013
Married	−.346	.339	.308
Years of education	.036	.047	.446
Dependents	−.027	.058	.638
Worked in agriculture	−.730 **	.295	.013
Worked in construction	.714 **	.307	.020
Sense of relative deprivation on scale of 1–10	129 ***	.049	.009
Number of migrations	052 *	.027	.056

The reference category is "no."
Statistically significant at the 99% (***$p < .01$), 95% (**$p < .05$) and 90% (*$p < .10$) confidence level.
N = 392.

A significant predictor of the intent to migrate is an individual's sense of relative deprivation, measured by the following question: "On a scale from 1 to 10, with 10 being the family with the best living conditions in this town, and 1 being the family with the poorest conditions, in which number would you put yourself and your family?" The higher a respondent self-rated, the more likely the respondent was to have reported the intent to migrate in 2005 (see table 3.8). This result might be a consequence of the high costs of migrating to the United States without documentation. The possibility of different opportunities to improve one's current economic situation through migration by definition would be associated with less impoverished individuals.

Another significant predictor of the intent to migrate was the sector that the respondent reported as their occupation. Interviewees who reported being in the construction sector were more likely to respond that they intended to migrate, while those who reported being in the agricultural sector were less likely to respond that they intended to migrate. This result illustrates that migrants from our research communities are responsive to sectoral dynamics in the receiving economy. With the United States experiencing a construction boom in 2005, the possibility of finding (or retaining) relatively high-paying construction jobs is higher and thus would justify the rising financial costs of migration.

Finally, the results also demonstrate that (1) males intend to migrate more than females, (2) respondents who had migrated more in the past were more likely to plan another trip during the next calendar year, and (3) as age increases, the likelihood of intent to migrate diminishes. Figure 3.2 illustrates the parabolic relationship between age and propensity to migrate among our interviewees.

Motives for Migration among Potential First-Timers

A full 30 percent of nonmigrants interviewed in our survey responded that they intended to migrate to the United States for the first time in 2005. Their motives (see table 3.9) mirror those cited by experienced migrants (table 3.6). Like experienced migrants, nearly three-fourths of first-time migrants cited economic reasons for wanting to migrate. "Push" factors in Mexico (economic necessity, no jobs in Mexico) accounted for 39.7 percent of these respondents, while "U.S. pull" factors (better pay, more jobs available in the United States) motivated 31.8 percent. These results support the general international migration hypothesis that migrants are both "pushed" out of their home countries and "pulled" into receiving countries because of the abundance of jobs and the availability of higher wages in the latter.

Figure 3.2. Propensity to Migrate, by Gender and Age

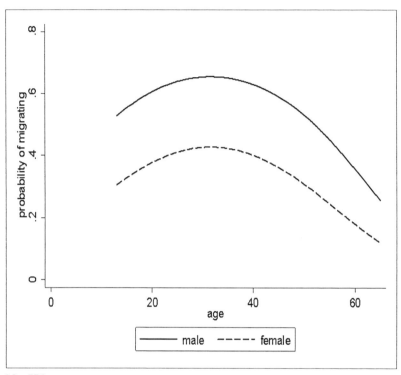

N = 556.

Table 3.9. Motives for Migration in 2005 among Potential First-Timers

Reason for Planning to Migrate in 2005	
Economic necessity	34.9%
Better pay in the United States	15.9%
More job opportunities in the U.S.	15.9%
No jobs available in Mexico	4.8%
All of the above: general economic rationale	71.5%
Family reunification	11.1%
Other	17.4%
Total	100.0%

N = 63.

Figure 3.3. Growth in Formal Employment in Jalisco and Zacatecas, 2003–2004

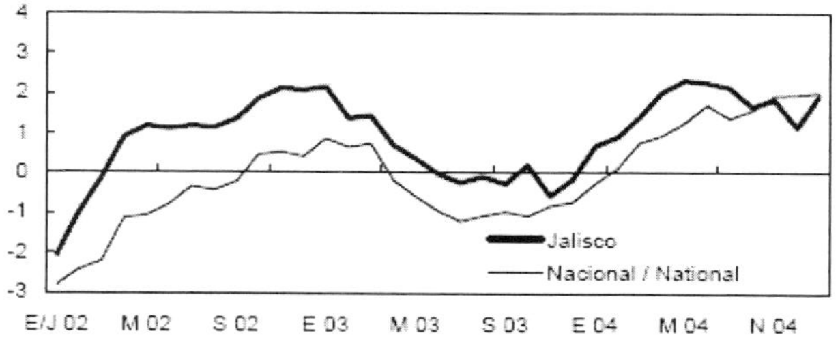

EMPLEO FORMAL / *FORMAL EMPLOYMENT* (IMSS)
Crecimiento anual / *Annual growth*, %

	Noviembre / *November*		Ene-Nov / *Jan-Nov*
	2003	2004	2004
Zacatecas	1.6	-1.3	1.4
Nacional / *National*	-0.8	2.0	1.2

Zacatecas
Nacional / National

EMPLEO FORMAL / *FORMAL EMPLOYMENT* (IMSS)
Crecimiento anual / *Annual growth*, %

	Noviembre / *November*		Ene-Nov / *Jan-Nov*
	2003	2004	2004
Jalisco	-0.6	1.9	1.7
Nacional / *National*	-0.8	2.0	1.2

Jalisco
Nacional / National

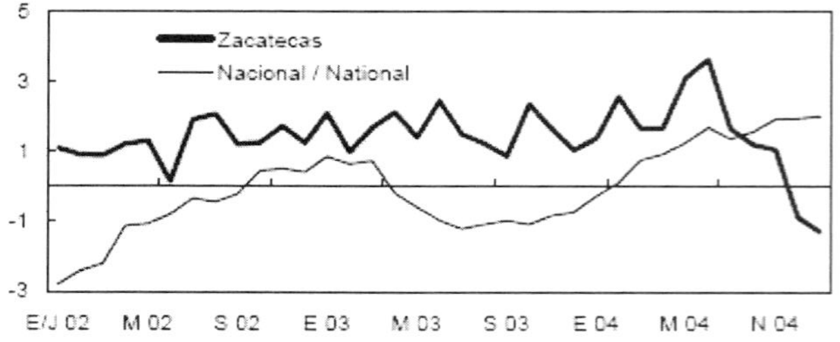

Source: Banamex, http://www.banamex.com/eng/esem/categoria.jsp?catalogo=Publications.

Figure 3.4. Annual Growth in Real Wages in Jalisco and Zacatecas, 2003–2004

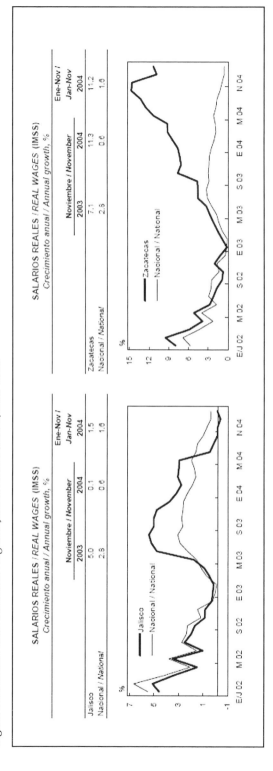

Source: Banamex, http://www.banamex.com/eng/esem/categoria.jsp?catalogo=Publications.

Macro-Economic Factors in Migration

In addition to feeling the effects of local economic conditions, residents of our research communities were also possibly being influenced by the macro-economic climates of their regions, states, and country. Nation-wide surveys conducted by Parametría (2005) found that among Mexicans who were actively seeking employment, 35 percent were considering migrating to the United States in November 2003, and by February 2005, 44 percent of job-seeking Mexicans were considering migration to the United States. The Mexican economy clearly is not generating enough jobs—especially well-paying ones—to deter migration. Concepción, who was cited earlier, lamented the state of the Mexican economy: "The Mexican economy is always in trouble. There are no jobs, and people have no one to work for. It's very difficult to survive."

Looking at economic indicators by state provides further insight into the factors driving migration from the region in which our research communities are located. For both states, employment growth rates generally have exceeded the national average in recent years (see figures 3.3 and 3.4). Zacatecas experienced a significantly higher growth rate in wages compared with the rest of the nation—11.6 percent versus a national rate of 1.6 percent. For the most part, Jalisco has paralleled or exceeded the national growth rate as well, only falling below the national average in the latter half of 2004. These data suggest that migrants from Tlacuitapa and Las Ánimas are being influenced more by local economic conditions or their perceptions of these conditions.

It is possible, of course, that wages in Tlacuitapa and Las Ánimas are on par with state averages but are still insufficient to hold people in their communities. Migration must be analyzed as a cumulative process in which the concept of *relative* deprivation plays a large role. When returning migrants visit their home communities, they display the consumer goods they have accumulated in "*el norte*," inspiring others to make the journey. Nazario, a nonmigrant from Tlacuitapa in his late 50s, complained: "Migrants, along with the lack of jobs, are to blame for young men leaving, because the migrants make life in the United States seem easy. They return home with money and with new cars and trucks." Even the relatively high wage and employment rates we find in Jalisco and Zacatecas cannot fully counter the allure of a better life in the United States.

CONCLUSIONS

Migration from our research communities is driven principally by economic considerations. The economic calculations that potential migrants make seem impervious to regional or national economic patterns. Rather, individuals make their migration decisions based almost exclusively on local economic conditions and their perceptions of these conditions. Transnational social networks are an indispensable resource for migrants who decide to cross the border. These networks facilitate the difficult transition from life in Mexico to life in the United States. Family and friends living in the United States guide new migrants in deciding where to migrate, help them settle, and assist them in finding employment.

References

Cohen, Jeffrey. 2004. *The Culture of Migration in Southern Mexico*. Austin: University of Texas Press.

Cornelius, Wayne. 1990. *Labor Migration to the United States: Development Outcomes and Alternatives in Mexican Sending Communities*. La Jolla: Center for U.S.-Mexican Studies University of California, San Diego.

Mines, Richard. 1981. *Developing a Community Tradition of Migration to the United States: A Field Study in Rural Zacatecas, Mexico, and California Settlement Areas*. La Jolla: Center for U.S.-Mexican Studies, University of California, San Diego.

Parametría. 2005. "Migración como alternativa al desempleo." May, http://parametria.com.mx/es_cartaext.php?id_carta=88.

Sherry, Adam. 2004. "Foundations of U.S. Immigration Control Policy: A Study of Information Transmission to Mexican Migrants and the Role of Information as a Deterrent at the Border." CCIS Working Paper No. 95. La Jolla, Calif.: Center for Comparative Immigration Studies, University of California, San Diego, http://www.ccis-ucsd.org/PUBLICATIONS/wrkg95.pdf.

4

Impacts of U.S. Immigration Policies on Migration Behavior

JEZMIN FUENTES, HENRY L'ESPERANCE, RAÚL PÉREZ, AND
CAITLIN WHITE

> *It was like I was already half dead. My third crossing lasted
> eight days. Scorpions, rattlesnakes, the river.... There were
> six of us, and thank God, the six of us made it through. On
> the sixth day we came across someone who was less fortu-
> nate. And who knows what he died of.*—Mejía, 52-year-old
> undocumented migrant from Tlacuitapa.

The preceding words from a seasoned undocumented migrant put a
human face on the struggles and emotional traumas migrants experience when crossing clandestinely into the United States. Many migrants
do not succeed on their first try, and some never make it across, yet
they keep trying. Undocumented immigration is a hot-button issue in
the United States, and both the Clinton and Bush administrations for-
mulated policies to stem the flow of illegal migrants. Beginning in early
1993 the Clinton administration steadily increased enforcement efforts
at the U.S.-Mexico border, significantly expanding the Border Patrol
and "securing" specific segments of the border. Over a decade later,
when it was abundantly clear that the border buildup had had little
impact on the overall numbers of undocumented immigrants entering
the U.S. labor market each year, the Bush administration proposed a
guestworker program to reduce illegal entries.

Although many observers have tried to predict and explain the
potential impacts of these policies, no previous study has explicitly
examined whether post-1993 border enforcement efforts have discour-

aged unauthorized Mexican migration at the individual level. Using evidence from our January 2005 study in Tlacuitapa and Las Ánimas, this chapter argues that the recent border enforcement buildup has not created a reliable deterrent to such migration. Although migrants perceive clandestine border crossings to be more dangerous, difficult, and costly than in the past, they continue to try—and succeed in—gaining entry. The Bush administration's proposal for a new guestworker program likewise has had little impact on migration decisions.

BORDER ENFORCEMENT AND THE PROPENSITY TO MIGRATE

Current U.S. immigration policy focuses almost exclusively on border enforcement as the most efficient method to stem undocumented immigration. Since 1993 this deterrence strategy has involved the deployment of additional personnel on the border and a more strategic use of deterrence technology. Concentrated Border Patrol operations such as "Hold the Line" in Texas (launched in 1993), "Gatekeeper" in California (begun in 1994), "Safeguard" in Arizona (begun in 1995), and "Rio Grande" in southern Texas (begun in 1998) aimed to deter undocumented migration at common points of entry. The Immigration and Naturalization Service (INS) and its successor, the Customs and Border Enforcement agency, have claimed that the enforcement strategies implemented by the Border Patrol since 1993 have reduced illegal immigration, pointing to sharp declines in apprehensions along heavily transited segments of the border like the San Diego and El Paso urban areas.

The following analysis challenges this claim. We find that while heightened border enforcement is keeping some people at home, it has not deterred the bulk of undocumented immigration into the United States. We argue that, in pursuing a border enforcement–centered strategy of immigration control, the U.S. government is assuming that an individual's decision to migrate is heavily influenced by the difficulty, danger, or cost of border crossing, ignoring the main factors that have been shown to drive Mexico-to-U.S. migration, which are overwhelmingly economic in nature (see chapter 3).

In order to assess the impact of increased border enforcement, we analyze the experiences and perceptions of undocumented migrants whose last border crossing occurred between 1993 and the time of our fieldwork in 2005. The first consideration is how much a migrant knows about enforcement efforts at the border prior to leaving the home community. Obviously, if a migrant does not know about the measures being taken by the U.S. government to secure the border, then these measures can have no effect on the decision to migrate. The majority of Tlacuitapeño and Animeño migrants we surveyed are aware of the recent border buildup. Seventy-five percent of our respondents who had crossed the border without documents between 1993 and 2004 reported that they were informed about the Border Patrol's vigorous efforts to intercept undocumented migrants. Yet 80.2 percent of these individuals reported that this knowledge did not influence their decision to migrate. A cross-tabulation between knowledge about border enforcement and intent to migrate in 2005 yielded no significant relationship ($N = 128; p = .722$).

The following comment helps to illustrate the extent of the knowledge that experienced as well as potential first-time migrants have regarding the dangers of clandestine border crossings. A widow whose husband died in the desert when trying to cross into Arizona in 1998 recalled a conversation with one of her sons, who had survived the same trip. Her son had told her:

> Mother, this same thing has been happening all along. It's just that, before, we had no way to see or hear the news. Now we can, and we constantly hear that someone has drowned or been killed while trying to cross. Like the guy that drowned at the Rio Grande; we saw that [on television], remember?

The son was referring to graphic images broadcast by the Mexican news network Eco of two migrants fighting for their lives and drowning in the unforgiving current of the Rio Grande River, with no rescue attempt made by the U.S. Border Patrol. The images underscored for everyone in Mexico the dangers of attempting a clandestine entry into the United States.

The risks at the border are not limited to drowning. The Border Patrol reported that the majority of the 373 migrant deaths detected in the U.S.-Mexico borderlands in fiscal year 2004 were caused by heat stroke or hypothermia. Of the undocumented migrants interviewed in Las Ánimas and Tlacuitapa who had crossed between 1993 and January 2005, 21.6 percent reported that they had suffered some physical pain or discomfort when crossing the border. Most commonly mentioned were fatigue, extreme cold, hunger, and dehydration. One experienced migrant from Tlacuitapa explained, "After three days in the desert, the blisters make it hard to keep on walking."

Undocumented migrants also risk becoming the victims of violent criminals. Martín, a 41-year-old migrant from Tlacuitapa who no longer wishes to return to the United States, described his experience with thieves in a 2001 border crossing:

> We were walking in a forest where there were lots of small trees; that's where the thieves came out of. They told us to hold still. They threatened us with a gun, then frisked us and took all our money…. They were like a gang from Mexico. We had not even crossed the border; we were still about one mile short of entering the United States.

In an even more dramatic example of the misfortunes that can befall undocumented border crossers, Alejandro, a 38-year-old Tlacuitapan and now a U.S. citizen, told how in 1998 a group of inexperienced migrants from Tlacuitapa asked him to accompany them across the Rio Grande to Acuna, Texas. Alejandro was already a seasoned crosser, so these men trusted that he could get them safely into the United States. Despite Alejandro's previous experience, four of the eleven men who attempted the crossing perished (two drowned, one died from dehydration, and one suffered severe head damage when he began to hallucinate and then fell). The remaining men barely survived.

Heightened border enforcement is not stopping undocumented entry, but it is clearly making it more difficult for undocumented migrants to enter the United States. Of the undocumented individuals in our 2005 survey who had crossed since 1993, 61.5 percent stated that they thought that crossing the border undetected was "much more difficult" than in previous years.[1] The two most common reasons given was the presence of more border agents (41.6 percent) and technological improvements that impede illegal entry, such as high-intensity lights (30.1 percent). Speaking of their own border-crossing experience, 47.2 percent of these post-1993 undocumented crossers stated that the crossing was harder than they had expected. Potential migrants who have never crossed the border agreed; 67.1 percent stated that, in their view, it was now much more difficult for an undocumented individual to cross undetected.[2]

Heightened border enforcement is also elevating the dangers to undocumented migrants. Undocumented individuals whose last border crossing was post-1993 feel that the border is more dangerous today; 78 percent judged it to be "very dangerous."[3] Among potential first-time migrants, 86.8 percent thought that illegal entry was very dangerous.[4]

Despite this increase in awareness of the difficulty and danger of clandestine border crossings, such perceptions showed no statistically significant relationship with a migrant's intention to go to the United States in 2005. Even if the migrant had himself suffered physical harm in his most recent border crossing, a cross-tabulation confirmed that such negative experiences were not affecting the decision to cross again in 2005.

To further test the hypothesis that border enforcement efforts can deter migration, we conducted a logit analysis of migration intention. Interviewees were asked if they were considering migrating in 2005; this variable was coded 1 for a positive response. To test the deterrent

---

[1] An additional 29.9 percent stated that it was somewhat more difficult. In total, 91.4 percent believed it was more difficult for an undocumented migrant to cross under present conditions.

[2] An additional 25.6 percent stated that it was somewhat more difficult. In total, 92.7 percent believed it was more difficult for an undocumented migrant to cross under present conditions.

[3] An additional 14.6 percent stated that it was somewhat dangerous. In total, 92.6 percent believed it was dangerous for an undocumented migrant to cross under present conditions.

[4] An additional 11.5 percent stated that it was somewhat dangerous. In total, 98.3 percent believed it was dangerous for an undocumented migrant to cross under present conditions.

Table 4.1. Probability of Migration Based on:

Pr(y=1) = f (deterrence, age, marital status, gender, education, number of children)
Documented and Undocumented Individuals

	Model 1 β	Model 2 β	Model 3 β	Model 4 β	Model 5 β	Model 6 β
Difficult	--	-0.050	--	--	--	0.005
		0.145				*0.150*
Border Patrol Info	--	--	0.613 ***	--	--	0.527 **
			0.202			*0.231*
Danger	--	--	--	-0.204	--	-0.294
				0.223		*0.278*
Death	--	--	--	--	1.000 ***	0.962 ***
					0.198	*0.218*
Gender	-0.931 ***	-0.812 ***	-0.920 ***	-0.894 ***	-0.915 ***	-0.732 ***
	0.214	*0.232*	*0.217*	*0.220*	*0.217*	*0.243*
Age	0.097 **	0.101 **	0.087 **	0.093 **	0.110 ***	0.104 **
	0.040	*0.042*	*0.041*	*0.040*	*0.040*	*0.043*
Age Squared	-0.002 ***	-0.002 ***	-0.001 ***	-0.001 ***	-0.002 ***	-0.002 ***
	0.000	*0.001*	*0.001*	*0.000*	*0.000*	*0.001*
Married	-0.041	-0.027	-0.082	-0.005	-0.227	-0.159
	0.251	*0.271*	*0.254*	*0.255*	*0.254*	*0.277*
Children	0.004	-0.001	0.005	0.001	0.000	-0.004
	0.048	*0.052*	*0.048*	*0.049*	*0.049*	*0.054*
Education	0.069 **	0.068 **	0.066 **	0.073 **	0.080 **	0.079 **
	0.032	*0.034*	*0.032*	*0.032*	*0.034*	*0.038*
Constant	-0.376	-0.449	-1.229	-0.265	-1.350	-2.161
	0.805	*0.965*	*0.857*	*0.820*	*0.838*	*1.086*
N	549	474	540	540	544	465
Wald Chi^2	46.550	38.020	52.100	45.180	67.240	56.600
Pr > Chi^2	0.000	0.000	0.000	0.000	0.000	0.000

Robust Standard Errors below coefficients in *italics*
*p<.1; **p<.05; ***p<.01 -- p-values are of two-tailed tests

effect of border enforcement, data on a number of border enforcement questions were included. First we included a dummy variable for whether the respondent believed that border enforcement efforts had made successful entry more difficult. Second, we included a three-part variable for the respondent's self-reported knowledge of border enforcement efforts (0 = none, 1 = some, 2 = a lot). Third, we included a variable for the individual's perceived risk of border crossing. This dichotomous variable was coded 1 if the potential migrant believed that crossing the border is very dangerous. We included a final dichotomous variable that measured whether the person knew someone who had died while attempting to cross the border, with the expectation that risk of death might serve as a deterrent. We also included a number of control variables: gender, a parabolic term for age, education, marital status, and number of children.

The results of our analysis show that gender, age, and education have important impacts on the propensity to migrate (see table 4.1). However, we could find no evidence that Border Patrol efforts actually deter undocumented migration. For all questions, the coefficient for this factor was either insignificant or in the opposite direction of the expected effect. People who had more information about border enforcement were *more* likely to cross, possibly because people planning to migrate seek out information about Border Patrol efforts.

Moreover, interviewees who knew someone who died while crossing the border are significantly *more* likely to risk a crossing themselves, indicating that even awareness of the risk of death does not deter entry. How to explain this counter-intuitive finding? Death at the border, while significant in terms of human impact, is a relatively low-frequency event relative to the thousands of people who cross each year, and would-be crossers seem to view this as an acceptable risk. The fact that this coefficient is positive and significant most likely indicates that people whose social cohort involves a large number of migrants are likely to cross themselves, and the larger the cohort of migrants, the more likely one member of the cohort is to have died while attempting illegal entry.

The data in table 4.1 are for our entire pool of interviewees, including both migrants and nonmigrants, but it may be more appropriate to ask if border enforcement strategies are influencing people who are likely to migrate. Table 4.2 includes data for individuals who reported having migrated at least once before; again, the dependent variable is intent to migrate in 2005. Isolating this group also allowed us to ask questions about the individual's previous migration experience. We included the same battery of control variables in this regression and added an additional control: whether the person had legal documents on the last visit to the United States. A person with documents clearly would not face the same risks and dangers as an undocumented migrant.

In this regression we included two variables to measure crossing difficulties. The first is a dummy variable coded 1 if the migrant reported having been apprehended at the border, and the second is another dichotomous variable coded 1 if the respondent reported that his/her last experience crossing the border was more difficult than expected. To get a sense of relative frequencies, 25 percent of the undocumented subjects reported that they had been caught at least once before, and 44 percent indicated that crossing was more difficult than anticipated.

The results in table 4.2 confirm that difficulty in crossing the border does not have a significant deterrent effect. Not surprisingly, people who have legal documents are almost six times more likely to report that they intend to enter the United States. However, controlling for documentation, age and martial status, previous apprehensions and perceived difficulties in crossing during the last attempt do not have a statistically significant impact on propensity to attempt entry again. Of the controls, we continue to find a parabolic relationship with respect to age.[5] Women are also found to be less likely to migrate, as are married people. In short, among the subset of respondents who are likely migrants, border enforcement efforts and perceived risks of crossing do not appear to play a large role in shaping migration decisions.

More than half (56.2 percent) of undocumented individuals whose last crossing was post-1993 planned to migrate in 2005. Intent to mi-

---

[5] The parabolic term was jointly significant in a likelihood ratio test at the .001 level.

grate was also common among potential first-timers: 29.9 percent of interviewees who had never gone north said they planned to do so in 2005. Among the 1993–2004 crossers and potential first-timers who were *not* planning to go to work in the United States in 2005, border enforcement was the most frequently cited reason for not migrating (23.1 and 14.5 percent, respectively, for recent crossers and potential first-timers), followed closely by family difficulties (see table 4.3). Thus border enforcement does have some measurable effect on people's propensity to migrate, although, as noted, when included in a multivariate analysis that effect is not statistically significant.

Table 4.2. Border Enforcement and Experienced Migrants' Propensity to Migrate

	Model 7 β	Model 8 β
Caught	−0.470	—
	0.364	
Prior difficulty	—	0.025
		0.337
Documented	1.745***	1.961***
	0.305	0.325
Gender	−0.540	−0.598*
	0.372	0.370
Age	0.100	0.120
	0.078	0.076
Age squared	−0.002**	−0.002**
	0.001	0.001
Married	−0.922**	−0.900**
	0.373	0.377
Children	0.041	0.041
	0.061	0.063
Education	−0.020	−0.016
	0.048	0.048
Constant	0.567	0.0037
	1.604	1.544
N	349	346
Wald Chi^2	70.940	68.040
Pr > Chi^2	0.000	0.000

Note: Robust standard errors below coefficients in *italics*.
*$p < 0.1$; **$p < 0.05$; ***$p < 0.01$, – p values are of two-tailed tests.

Table 4.3. Motives for *Not* Migrating to the United States in 2005

Reason Given	Experienced Undocumented Migrants Who Last Crossed Post-1993[a] (%)	Potential First-time Migrants[b] (%)
More difficult to cross	23.1	14.5
Not interested	1.9	14.5
Family difficulties	19.2	12.2
No economic need	17.3	11.5
Age (too old)	3.8	6.9
Age (too young)	—	6.9
Lack of money to pay for trip	3.8	6.1
Sees possibility to improve life at home	11.5	5.3
Has to finish studies	1.9	5.3
Has friends/family at home	3.8	3.8
Doesn't like life in U.S.	3.8	2.3
Has job in Mexico	—	2.3
Illness	1.9	2.3
Is used to life in Mexico	—	1.5
Doesn't know	—	1.5
Other	7.7	3.1
Total	100.0	100.0

[a] N = 53; [b] N = 131.

IMPACTS OF BORDER ENFORCEMENT ON PEOPLE-SMUGGLING

> *Coyotes roam all over the border, but they are not to be trusted because how does one know that a coyote is good? I pay a bit more to have a secure crossing. I already have a trustworthy coyote, and he knows what is happening at Tijuana/San Ysidro, so I no longer need to ask around for one.*

One result of increased border enforcement has been migrants' increased reliance on professional people-smugglers (*coyotes*) to cross the border. Although hiring a *coyote* is expensive, many undocumented migrants use them in hopes of reducing the risk of apprehension by the

Border Patrol. Reliance on *coyotes* and *coyotes'* fees has risen on par with the likelihood of apprehension at the border and the level of danger involved in a clandestine border crossing. *Coyotes* are very knowledgeable about border enforcement, and many have developed considerable skill in evading Border Patrol agents. As discussed below, stepped-up border enforcement has increased the use of *coyotes,* inflated *coyote* fees, and pushed migrant crossings eastward into new and hostile terrain. The migrants' extensive utilization of *coyotes* helps explain why tougher border enforcement has failed to halt the growth of the U.S. undocumented immigrant population: professionally assisted crossings are more likely to be successful.

Use of *Coyotes*

People-smuggling has long been a part of unauthorized migration to the United States. López Castro (1998) identified three types of *coyotes*: local-interior, local-border, and border-business. Local-interior *coyotes* reside in the migrant-sending communities. They cross migrants a few at a time and on foot, and then help them link up with a train or bus that will take them to their final destination. Local-interior *coyotes* charge the least and are the most trusted. Local-border *coyotes* live on the border but are natives of migrant-sending communities and primarily serve migrants from their own hometowns. They travel with larger groups of migrants, often use a vehicle to take them across the border, and charge a higher fee.

Finally, border-business *coyotes* reside at the border and recruit aspiring migrants. These *coyotes* carry out sophisticated operations in collaboration with individuals at various ports of entry, and they may also rent or sell fake documents to the migrants. Some interviewees in Tlacuitapa recounted how their *coyote* had crossed them through a particular car lane at the Tijuana/San Diego border crossing; the *coyote* had arranged for the border inspector in that lane to accept their fake documents as valid and allow the undocumented passengers into the United States. Border-business *coyotes* put migrants in "safe houses" once they have crossed the border. Border-business *coyotes* charge the highest fees and move the largest numbers of migrants. Because they are based at the border, they can keep up to date on Border Patrol tactics and develop strategies to evade them. The majority of undocumented migrants from our two research communities prefer to obtain a *coyote* through family or friends (see figure 4.1). Nevertheless, a significant share (31 percent) simply come to the border and look for an unknown *coyote* there.

Figure 4.1. How Undocumented Migrants Contact *Coyotes*

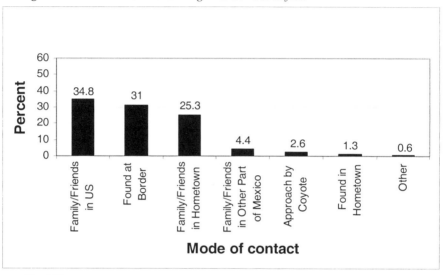

N = 158.

We spoke to many experienced migrants in 2005 who reported that they continued to use *coyotes* despite having gained personal knowledge of border-crossing strategies on previous trips to the United States. Francisco, a 32-year-old migrant from Tlacuitapa, explained:

> Why risk it? I would rather pay more to ensure my security. One never knows what they [the *coyotes*] know; they have all the information. Plus, I always use the same *coyote*; I trust him because he charges me according to what I need and where I want to go.

Although some undocumented migrants attempt to cross unassisted, the vast majority now rely on *coyotes*. *Coyote* usage in our research communities has increased during the post-1993 period of tighter border enforcement. Prior to 1993, 78 percent of undocumented migrants crossed with a *coyote* (see figure 4.2). For undocumented migrants who crossed from 1993 to the time of our interviews in 2005, 90 percent used *coyotes*. Looking at undocumented crossers on a year-to-year basis since 1993 (figure 4.3), we find that only a very small percentage of migrants have dared to cross alone.

Figure 4.2. Undocumented Migrants' Use of *Coyotes*, 1967–1992 and 1993–2004[a]

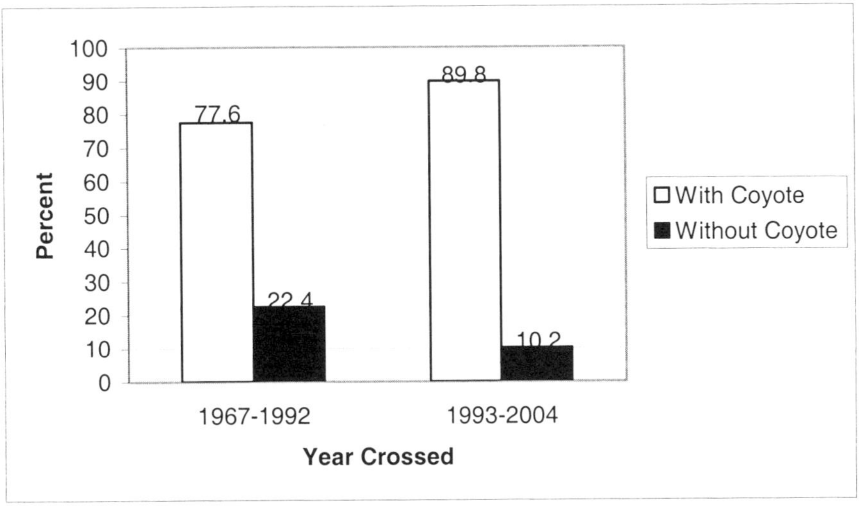

N = 185.
[a] Based on the last time a migrant crossed the border (1967 is the earliest "last year crossed" from the previous survey).

Despite the increased use of *coyotes* since 1993, significant numbers of people are still being apprehended by Border Patrol agents (over one million apprehensions are now being made annually). This is indicative of the increased difficulty associated with crossing into the United States, even with a *coyote*. However, the vast majority of our interviewees who crossed clandestinely during the post-1993 period were not apprehended (see figure 4.4), and 92 percent of those who were apprehended attempted the crossing again on the same trip to the border, succeeding in entering on the second or third try.

Figure 4.3. Undocumented Migrants' Use of *Coyotes*, 1993–2004[a]

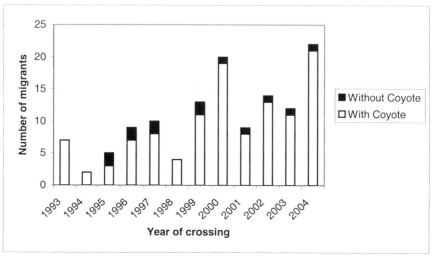

N = 127.
[a] Based on last year a migrant crossed.

Figure 4.4. Percentage of Undocumented Migrants Apprehended, 1967–2004[a]

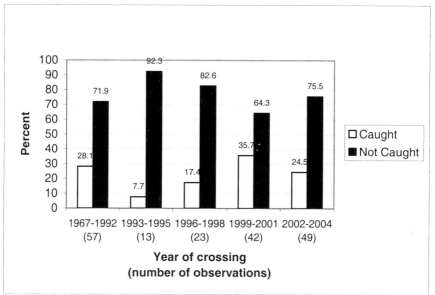

N = 184.
[a] Based on last year a migrant crossed.

Rising *Coyote* Fees

As undocumented migrants have become increasingly dependent on *coyotes* to cross a more heavily fortified border, *coyotes*—having excellent business sense—have raised their fees. Whereas the median fee paid to a *coyote* in the ten years prior to the 1993 border buildup was $613, the median fee had almost tripled—to $1,634—for migrants who crossed most recently between 2002 and 2004 (figure 4.5). Correspondingly, the total cost of clandestine entry (including *coyote* fees, travel to the border, and so on) has more than doubled (figure 4.6).

Figure 4.5. Fees Migrants Paid to *Coyotes* on Most Recent Trip, 1982–2004

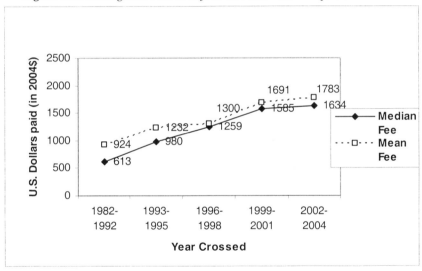

N = 128.

U.S.-bound undocumented migrants finance their trips in a variety of ways. Some use personal savings, which are often dollars earned during a previous stint in the United States. Many undocumented immigrants depend on financial help from family or friends in the United States or in their home community. Mirna, a shoe factory worker from Tlacuitapa, explained the difficulty she encountered in trying to finance her trip to the United States:

I have not left because I do not have enough money to pay for a *coyote*; I need money to make it. I cannot count on money in hand, but I count on loaned money from the United States. My family members who are there will pay for me.... The *coyote* will cost $1,500, and half is paid here in Mexico and the rest once I have crossed into the United States. All of my family's migration has been done in the same way, from money that they save from working in the United States.

Figure 4.6. Total Cost of Most Recent Unauthorized Trip to the U.S., 1982–2004

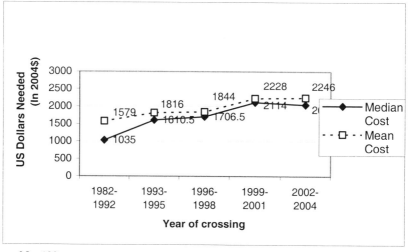

N = 139.

Although the cost of a *coyote* is high, undocumented migrants have every incentive to pay top dollar to avoid a bad experience at the border. Martín, the Tlacuitapan migrant quoted earlier, told how his group was abandoned by a *coyote* they had hired at a bargain price:

He left us in the middle of nowhere; we had to continue our journey alone, asking ourselves where he was. You don't know what's going to happen; people begin to run all over the place. Maybe some tagged along with the *coyote*, but he left us behind. We found bodies along the path. It was a rough experience.

The increase in *coyotes'* fees is partially due to their need to develop more creative and more expensive methods to get their clients across a more heavily enforced border. For example, Antonia, a 31-year-old mother from Tlacuitapa, recounted that she and her 8-year-old daughter crossed through the Tijuana/San Ysidro port of entry stuffed inside a mattress; Antonia paid $1,300 for their risky yet successful crossing.

Coyotes often have established relationships with officials at key points of entry that enable them to cross migrants more safely and effectively but at an additional cost. In May 2001, several INS inspectors and Border Patrol agents on the international bridge between Matamoros and Brownsville, Texas, were found to be accepting payments of $350 to $500 to pass cars through the port of entry without inspecting documents (Benavidez 2001; Burnett 2001; Garrido 2001; Méndez Martínez 2001; Negrete Lares 2001). The case was not an isolated incident. On June 8, 2005, the *San Diego Union-Tribune* reported that an anticorruption unit at the San Ysidro border checkpoint was indicted—ironically—on corruption charges, accused of accepting money from Mexican smugglers (Soto 2005). As long as *coyotes* can rely on corrupt Mexican and U.S. border officials to wave them through, they will continue to use these more expensive crossing options and simply pass the cost along to the undocumented migrants who pay for their services.

Shifting Points of Entry

Data from our 2005 survey reveal shifts in points of entry for undocumented migrants between 1967 and 2005 (see figure 4.7). Prior to the 1993 implementation of stricter border enforcement, the California border was the leading point of entry (with 74.1 percent of undocumented crossers passing through this state), but beginning in 1993 there was a rise in the proportion of undocumented migrants entering through Arizona and a corresponding drop in the numbers entering through California. Among our interviewees who had migrated illegally between 1993 and 2005, 45.6 percent had entered through California and 24.8 percent through Arizona.

Figure 4.7. Points of Entry of Undocumented Migrants, 1967–2004[a]

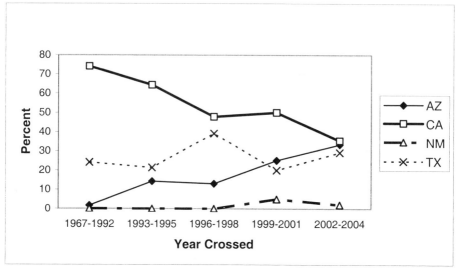

N = 183.
[a] Based on last year a migrant crossed; Chi square = .002.

As discussed in chapter 3, the final destinations of migrants from our research communities have shifted as new immigrant networks have developed in various U.S. states. However, part of the shift away from California and toward Arizona can also be attributed to the fact that hardened enforcement along key stretches of the California-Mexico border has shifted *coyotes* and migrants eastward, where the physical environment is more hostile but the border is less strictly guarded. In many places along the Arizona-Mexico border, a three-foot barbwire fence is all that divides the two countries. Rodolfo, an experienced migrant from Tlacuitapa, describes the lucrative business of crossing migrants in these remote areas:

> *Coyotes* in these areas are recommended by migrants who've already used them to cross the border there. These *coyotes* make more money than drug dealers, because many of them take fifty to sixty people at a time, charging $2,000 per person, and they cross an average of three times a week. They have ways of crossing so many people at a time.

THE IMPACT OF A PROPOSED TEMPORARY WORKER PROGRAM

In early 2004 President George W. Bush proposed a new temporary worker program that would "match willing foreign workers with willing U.S. employers." Some observers suggest that Bush's proposal has encouraged illegal immigration by people (mainly Mexicans) who are under the false impression that they will gain automatic U.S. citizenship through this guestworker program. However, the results from our 2005 survey in Tlacuitapa and Las Ánimas, which included specific questions about the Bush proposal, indicate that such fears have little basis. Following a brief overview of President Bush's proposed guestworker program, this section discusses the relevant results from our research communities.

The Bush program would offer an unlimited number of visas for foreign workers who are matched with jobs in the United States. The stated goal is to offer temporary legal status to the millions of undocumented migrants who enter the United States every year in search of work, while simultaneously satisfying the labor demand of employers who often cannot find willing U.S. workers. To get a work visa, a potential migrant would need to present a letter or affidavit from an employer certifying a job offer or an ongoing employment relationship. The foreign worker would be able to apply for the job from either the United States or his or her home country. Undocumented workers applying from within the United States would have to pay a fine (because of their current illegal status), but they would be able to continue working, assuming a U.S. employer wished to hire them.

Under Bush's proposal, holders of these visas could work legally in the United States for between three and six years, but they would be required to return to their home country upon the visa's expiration unless they had obtained permanent legal status in the interim. Despite allegations to the contrary, Bush's proposed guestworker program offers no automatic path to U.S. citizenship. Workers holding temporary visas under the program would have to follow the same procedures as anyone else to attain permanent legal resident status and eventually U.S. citizenship. Although guestworkers could apply for a "green card" as soon as they received the temporary worker visa, they would be placed at the end of the queue and thus have no advantage over other green-card seekers. Under Bush's proposal, an individual with a temporary work visa could bring his or her dependents to the United States, but the dependents could not be employed unless they also obtained temporary work visas.

As noted above, many observers—including some Border Patrol agents—have claimed that President Bush's proposal has encouraged heavier illegal immigration, but for this to occur, migrants would need to be aware of the proposal and its specifics. We found that among experienced undocumented migrants from Tlacuitapa and Las Ánimas, only 55.4 percent had any knowledge of the proposal, and 70.3 percent of potential first-time migrants had never heard of it. Among whose who had heard of the proposal, 58 percent of undocumented migrants and 61.7 percent of potential first-timers correctly identified it as a new guestworker program. However, less than 10 percent in each group knew the length of time that the work permits would be valid.

For both experienced and potential first-time undocumented migrants, cross-tabulations found no significant relationship between intent to migrate in 2005 and knowledge of the Bush proposal. In terms of actual migration behavior, only one of our interviewees reported that his most recent trip to the United States had been motivated primarily by the Bush proposal. Further, only 17 percent of experienced undocumented migrants and 36.2 percent of potential migrants who knew about the proposal said they knew someone else who had gone to the United States to take advantage of it. And only 21.7 percent of potential migrants and 27 percent of experienced undocumented migrants with some knowledge of the proposal believed that participation in the program would lead to legalization. When we asked respondents what they would need to do to legalize their stay in the United States under the Bush proposal (a trick question of sorts), the majority did not know, and only 8.9 percent of experienced undocumented migrants and 8.7 percent of potential migrants correctly stated that it is not possible to legalize through this program. The majority responded that an individual must apply for a green card, which points toward legal residency, not citizenship.

CONCLUSION

We find that stronger border enforcement has not significantly reduced unauthorized migration to the United States from our research communities. Rather, tighter border controls have increased the costs of undocumented immigration by increasing migrants' reliance on *coyotes*, whose rising fees, in turn, reflect the need to devise more creative, and sometimes more expensive, ways to cross people over the border. Heightened border enforcement at key points of entry has also contributed to a shift in entry points from California to Arizona and Texas, where harsh topographical and climatic conditions raise the likelihood of physical suffering and even death.

References

Benavidez, Rachel. 2001. "Smuggling Case Goes to Grand Jury," *Brownsville Herald*, May 25.

Burnett, John. 2001. "Immigrant Smugglers." Segment on National Public Radio's *Morning Edition*, June 22.

Garrido, Ernie J. 2001. "INS Inspectors' Arraignments Set," *Brownsville Herald*, June 13.

López Castro, Gustavo. 1998. "Coyotes and Alien Smuggling." In *Binational Study: Migration between Mexico and the United States*, vol. 3: *Research Reports and Background Materials*. Mexican Ministry of Foreign Relations and the U.S. Commission on Immigration Reform, http://www.utexas.edu/lbj/uscir/binpapers/v3a-6lopez.pdf.

Méndez Martínez, Georgina. 2001. "Los 'migra-pateros' se declaran inocentes," *El Mañana*, June 14.

Negrete Lares, Ángeles. 2001. "Otro inspector del INS acusado de patero," *El Nuevo Heraldo*, June 9.

Soto, Onell. 2005. "Ex-Border Officials Face Charges of Corruption," *San Diego Union-Tribune*, June 8.

5

U.S. Settlement Behavior and
Labor Market Participation

Henry López, Rob Oliphant, and Edith Tejeda

> *Yes, I would like my daughter to study over there [in the United States] so she could see what a good school is like, but to live there, no. That may be for some, but not for me.*—Rodolfo, non-migrant in Tlacuitapa.

> *I remember what this place used to be like ... how the people got together to have a drink, to hold dances. There was more activity and all. The people used to have more energy, more drive. But they all sold up and moved away, whole families. They have land here, but they sell it and they leave.*—Pablo, experienced U.S. migrant in Tlacuitapa.

In today's climate of fervent anti-immigration sentiment in the United States, the presence and permanency of immigrants within U.S. society stirs a good deal of interest. Many scholars have studied migrants' settlement patterns and their participation in the labor market, but recent developments—such as "Operation Gatekeeper," a resurgence of anti-immigrant legislation, and fluctuations in the U.S. economy—have changed the context in which migrant settlement behavior is occurring. In theory, state and local immigration control measures such as Arizona's Proposition 200 should decrease the number of undocumented immigrants settling permanently in the United States. However, as discussed below, immigrants' resourcefulness, persistence, and ability to innovate often produce unexpected policy outcomes.

In the analysis of our 2005 survey results presented here, we use place of primary residence as a proxy for settlement. That is, we assume that migrants who were considered to be based primarily in the United States at the time of interview are more likely to settle permanently in that country than those who continue to spend most of their time in the home community. Of course, we cannot conclusively determine the extent of settlement in the United States by migrants from our research communities, given that we conducted our fieldwork only in the sending communities and thus could not interview people who had decided to remain in the United States and not return for their hometowns' annual fiestas. Given this limitation, we consider place of primary residence to be the best indicator of our interviewees' future settlement behavior.

This chapter focuses on border enforcement and on migrants' employment and use of social services in the United States, analyzing their impacts on migrants' tendency to settle in the United States. Although many of these factors, such as border fortification and scale-backs in social services, are intended to control immigration at the border or in the interior, they also create unintended consequences that could influence settlement in the United States. We first try to determine to what extent migrants' decisions to settle in the United States or Mexico can be attributed to border enforcement. We argue that the fortification of the U.S.-Mexico border has been more effective in preventing undocumented migrants from returning to Mexico than in preventing them from entering the United States.

Given that many working-age migrants come to the United States in search of employment opportunities and higher wages, we next examine how certain jobs and income levels affect decisions to settle. We discuss the role that employers and social networks play in channeling immigrant workers to certain jobs, as well as whether laws designed to restrict immigrants' ability to work in the United States are having an effect.

For migrants in the United States, especially those whose families have joined them, integration into U.S. society may entail the use of social services, especially education and health care. This has led many politicians to claim that immigrants are unfairly and purposefully draining taxpayer-supported social services. However, an analysis of our survey results on migrants' use of primary public benefits, as well as the level of their tax contribution and the legal status of recipients of social services, raises serious questions about the usefulness of measures that restrict immigrants' access to social services as an instrument for reducing "unwanted" immigration.

EMPTYING OUT A COMMUNITY

A count of unoccupied homes illustrates the rate at which whole families have left Tlacuitapa to relocate to the United States. Over the course of two weeks, our research team visited and revisited every house in Tlacuitapa in order to interview household members. If we were unable to locate anyone at home after multiple visits, we asked neighbors where the families had relocated and how long they had been gone.

A comparison of the number of unoccupied houses recorded in a 1995 survey of the town with what we found in January 2005 confirms a trend from individual migration to whole-family movement to the United States. In 1995, there were thirty-six uninhabited houses in Tlacuitapa; the majority of their former residents had migrated to California, Oklahoma, or Nevada, and a few had left for other parts of Mexico. A decade of migration had added more than one hundred vacant houses to this count; in 2005 we counted 138 vacant houses in Tlacuitapa.

Tlacuitapa's natives have come to accept this exodus as characteristic of their town's present and future. Rubén, who had witnessed eighty years of Tlacuitapa's history, supported the individuals who chose to leave the town: "From childhood they think about going to the other side; now there is nothing here, not even for an old man like me." Rubén's comments underscore the reality that there are few opportunities in Tlacuitapa that surpass the hope of success in the United States, and it would be naïve to expect this to change in the near future. The increase in the number of abandoned homes suggests the degree to which this town's migrants are planting roots and settling in the United States. Some of the houses lie abandoned, others are occupied for a week or two when migrants return for the town's annual fiestas, and many are intended to be retirement homes for their owners who are currently working in the United States.

THE EFFECTS OF BORDER FORTIFICATION

Although the intended aim of stepped-up U.S. border enforcement efforts, such as California's "Operation Gatekeeper," is to reduce the number of undocumented immigrants entering the United States, such strategies may also have had the unintended consequence of encouraging already-present undocumented migrants to settle in the United States rather than risk apprehension at the border. After weighing the costs and benefits of an illegal border crossing to gain reentry to the United States, undocumented individuals seem less ready than in the past to return to their hometowns for the annual fiestas or to reunite with their families. This represents a reversal in the historical pattern; in the past most Mexican immigrants came to the United States to work for a limited time, after which they returned to Mexico until a time that they decided to migrate temporarily once again.

A migrant's decision to settle in the United States takes account of a number of factors, including increased vigilance at the border and the logistics of their cross-border journeys. When we asked undocumented migrants from Tlacuitapa and Las Ánimas whether, on their last sojourn to the United States, they stayed the length of time they had expected, more than a third (36.7 percent) said that they had stayed longer. The reasons they gave for extending their time in the United States were, first, economic necessity and, second, increased border enforcement. That is, they preferred to remain longer rather than return home and then have to risk a second illegal entry (see table 5.1).

Table 5.1. Reasons Why Undocumented Migrants Stayed Longer Than Expected on Most Recent Trip to the United States

Reason Given	Percent
Economic necessity	52.2
Border enforcement	14.5
Family reasons	14.5
Illness (self or family)	5.8
Other	12.1
Total	99.1

N = 69.

Extending one's stay may also be a response to the rising costs associated with traveling to and from Mexico. Among our interviewees who have legal documents to live and work in the United States and who give the United States as their primary place of residence, 78.6 percent stated that they return to their home community at least once a year. In contrast, only 35.9 percent of migrants without documents stated that they return home once a year. In other words, Mexican migrants who have proper documentation are more mobile between the two countries and thus are better able to maintain contact with their home community. And for undocumented migrants, the weakening in community ties that comes about because they are not able to maintain such close contact with their hometowns further increases the likelihood that they will settle permanently in the United States.

As further confirmation of this trend, while only 12.9 percent of migrants who are in the United States legally and give this country as their primary base responded that their visits to their hometowns in Mexico are less frequent now than in previous years, 37.8 percent of undocumented individuals said that this was the case. The most common reasons that undocumented migrants from Tlacuitapa and Las Ánimas gave to explain the decreased frequency of their visits to their hometowns in Mexico were all associated with border enforcement; 82.4 percent of undocumented migrants offered one of the following: the difficulty of evading "La Migra," rising costs (including *coyote* fees), and a heightened sense of the dangers entailed in clandestine border crossings.

Among our informants who have documented status in the United States, half cited work obligations as the reason for the reduced frequency of their visits to the home community. Employment also contributes to the settlement decision because a steady job enhances the possibility of creating a sustainable life in the United States, as discussed later in this chapter. Another variable that plays into the settlement decision is the number of family members already living in the United States. Having an ample support network of relatives in the United States can ease the transition from life in Mexico to life in America.

THE EFFECTS OF LABOR POLICIES, EMPLOYMENT, AND INCOME ON SETTLEMENT BEHAVIOR

In 1986 the United States passed the Immigration Control and Reform Act (IRCA), claiming that it would lessen immigration by punishing employers who "knowingly" hire unauthorized migrants. Numerous immigration scholars have confirmed the importance of employment for settlement behavior. For example, Leo Chávez showed that income and steady employment are the most important factors influencing settlement (Chávez 1992, 1994). Rafael Alarcón determined that the number of years a migrant has lived in the United States and changes in the U.S. economy affect settlement decisions (in Torres Sarmiento 2002: 29). And Wayne Cornelius (1992: 157) has argued that immigration from Mexico has become more permanent since the 1980s because of the following factors: (1) changes in the U.S. economy that have affected the nature and magnitude of the demand for Mexican immigrant labor; (2) recurrent economic crises in Mexico; (3) IRCA; and (4) the maturation of transnational migrant networks. Cornelius calls attention to the importance of sociocultural factors, such as family reunification, in settlement behavior. While Mexico-to-U.S. migration formerly comprised mostly working-age men, women and children are now joining husbands, fathers, other relatives, and friends, reuniting their families and making settlement in the United States a more desirable option.

This section focuses on the role that employment, income, and social networks play in a migrant's decision to settle permanently in the United States. We draw on previous studies and on our findings from the 2005 fieldwork in Tlacuitapa and Las Ánimas to demonstrate the ineffectiveness of IRCA, particularly employer sanctions, in curtailing the entry and permanent settlement of Mexican migrants.

Employer Sanctions

There are two key questions regarding IRCA's employer sanctions provision. First, are employer sanctions being enforced? And second, are they affecting migrants' perceptions of the ease or difficulty of finding work? According to Cornelius, "for IRCA to have the kinds of long-term consequences that its proponents intended, the law will have to change well-established perceptions, behavior patterns, and socialization processes in the principal source areas for unauthorized migration to the United States" (Cornelius 1990: 227). IRCA's success can be gauged, then, by determining whether potential and experienced migrants believe that it is difficult to find work in the United States. That is, has IRCA dissuaded undocumented migrants already in the United States and potential future migrants still in Mexico from seeking work in the United States? If employer sanctions made it harder to find work, undocumented migrants already in the United States would return to Mexico and spread the word to those who have not yet migrated.

Our findings indicate that migrants' decisions to settle permanently in the United States were not affected by any perception that finding a job would be difficult. Among undocumented experienced migrants, 69.1 percent of those who were based primarily in Tlacuitapa or Las Ánimas responded that it was more difficult to find work now than in the past, and 60.5 percent of those based principally in the United States said the same. The difference in these groups' responses is not statistically significant. Interestingly, these figures are far below what Cornelius had found in his 1989 survey of Tlacuitapa and Las Ánimas, when 83 percent of interviewed household heads and recent migrants believed that it was more difficult than before to get work in the United States because of employer sanctions (Cornelius 1990: 230).

Another indication that employer sanctions may not significantly increase migrants' perceptions about their ability to find work in the United States is the fact that very few of our interviewees had been asked for documentation by their U.S. employers. Forty-four percent of our undocumented respondents reported that they were not required to provide proof of legal status to their most recent employer; among documented migrants, the number was 24 percent. Construction was first among the industries that did not ask for work authorization (40 percent of undocumented construction workers reported not having had to provide documents), followed by agriculture. Overall, these findings demonstrate that many employers, especially those who are heavily dependent on cheap immigrant labor, are not taking serious steps to confirm the immigration status of their workers.

Employment/Income of Migrants Living Primarily in the United States

The question of whether to return to Mexico or settle in the United States has been linked to a migrant's ability to find work and also to the quality of the job he or she obtains. In an analysis of data from the Mexican Migration Project, Belinda Reyes examined duration of stay in the United States among undocumented migrants and found that "for men the odds of return migration are greatest for those who are unemployed … [and] skilled workers were the least likely to return" (Reyes 2004: 314). Supporting Reyes's findings, Fernando Riosmena found that "the likelihood of return is contingent on occupation in the United States" (2004: 275). Riosmena also added "cumulative U.S. experience" to the list of factors, reflecting the fact that the longer a migrant works in the United States, the more likely he or she will have a job that pays well, hence making it more likely that the migrant will settle permanently. Although our findings did not reveal a correlation between employment in a particular industry and likelihood of settlement, they suggest that a related factor, income, may be important.

Within our survey sample, the largest fraction of those who said that they resided primarily in the United States were employed in construction: 60 percent of undocumented and 44 percent of documented respondents. Only 6.3 percent of our undocumented interviewees and 5.9 percent of the documented respondents were employed in agriculture. Even though a growing percentage of U.S.-bound migrants from our research communities work in construction (as discussed in chapter 3), a construction job does not increase the likelihood that a migrant will decide to remain in the United States. In fact, immigrants in our survey sample who worked primarily in construction were more likely to be living primarily in Tlacuitapa or Las Ánimas than in the United States. Large numbers of migrants working in U.S. agriculture are also returning to Mexico.

As noted earlier, while there is a general shift toward construction as the preferred sector of employment among Tlacuitapeños and Animeños working in the United States, there is little evidence that finding a job in construction (or any other specific industry) influences migrants' settlement decisions. Among undocumented migrants who now live primarily in Tlacuitapa or Las Ánimas, 45.5 percent reported having worked in construction during their most recent U.S. sojourn; although this fraction is lower than the corresponding number among undocumented migrants living principally in the United States (58.3 percent), it is surprisingly similar. There is a broad range of salaries for jobs that male migrants (documented and undocumented) fill in the construction category. Most immigrant construction workers in our sample (51.9 percent of undocumented and 69.4 percent of documented) had earned between US$1,501 and $2,000 a month. We found 20.4 percent of undocumented construction workers and 11.3 percent of documented construction workers at the lower end of the wage scale (salaries between $500 and $1,000 a month). This disparity in wages within the construction sector (and similar sectors) may explain why many immigrant workers opt to return to their homeland.

Income may be a better indicator of whether a migrant will decide to reside primarily in the United States. Assuming that most documented migrants of working age generally reside in the United States and have significantly higher income levels, we looked exclusively at the relationship between income and place of residence for undocumented migrants. There was a stark difference in income among those who stated they were undocumented during their last trip and live primarily in Mexico and those who were undocumented on the last trip and live primarily in the United States. Generally speaking, undocumented migrants with higher incomes are more likely to live principally in the United States. Of course, higher wages may encourage settlement in the United States, or higher wages may be the result of having settled in the United States. The mean salary in the United States for a migrant whose primary residence is in Tlacuitapa was $1,273, while the mean salary for migrants whose primary residence is in the United States was $1,605 (see table 5.2).

The relationships between undocumented status, income, and principal place of residence yielded very high significance levels. However, the cause of this differentiation in income and place of residence is not readily apparent. It is possible that higher-paying employment provides an incentive for the migrant to remain in the United States. Yet it could also be the case that the networks that allow a migrant to stay longer in the United States also assist him to find better jobs.

Table 5.2. Reported U.S. Salary of Undocumented Migrants,
by Principal Place of Residence

Salary per Month (in US$)	Primary Residence in United States (N = 180)	Primary Residence in Mexico (N = 184)
$1–$500	0.6%	1.1%
$501–$1,000	13.9%	35.9%
$1,001–$1,500	34.4%	38.1%
$1,501–$2,000	45.0%	23.9%
$2,001–$2,500	3.3%	0.5%
$2,501–$3,000	1.1%	0.0%
$3,000 & greater	1.7%	0.5%
Mean salary per month	$1,605	$1,273

Role of Social Networks in the Settlement Process

The social networks that have grown up between Mexicans living in the United States and their families and friends in Mexico serve to relay information and to provide help at both ends of the migration circuit. Cornelius found that among immigrants living in San Diego County in 1996, 70 percent of undocumented workers had found their current job through a relative or friend employed at the same firm where they now worked (Cornelius 1998: 144). Our data confirm that social networks are crucial resources for finding employment for migrants from Tlacuitapa and Las Ánimas. Because the undocumented are the most vulnerable migrants, they relied most heavily on friends and family for finding work. Seventy percent of documented migrants stated that they found work through their social networks; 88 percent of undocumented migrants reported doing so.

The strength of social networks has been linked to the likelihood of permanent settlement. According to Belinda Reyes, "originating from a family with a significant migration experience reduced the probability of going home, even if other household members were present illegally in the United States.... In general, there has been a decrease over time in the probability of return among those residing in households with large migrant networks" (Reyes 2004: 314). Our findings suggest that for migrants from Tlacuitapa and Las Ánimas, the number of relatives living in the United States significantly influences settlement in the United States. These communities' long histories of migration have ensured that virtually everyone from Tlacuitapa and Las Ánimas has relatives living in the United States with whom they could live for relatively long periods or even permanently.

Although most people in our study claimed to have many relatives living in the United States, an extended family network in the United States does not by itself guarantee that a migrant will decide to settle there permanently. Many undocumented migrants with relatives in the United States have been able to cross the border and find work, but they then face a life apart from their spouses and children. Martín, a man in his mid-thirties who has migrated several times but whose family has always remained in Mexico, describes why he decided to return to Tlacuitapa rather than move his family to the United States:

> There are families that go to the United States, and they return because they don't make it over there. Living over there and living here is the same thing because the family needs to be supported. And there are times that they can't even afford to pay rent [in the United States] with what they earn.

This case illustrates the importance of an adequate income as a key factor in settlement decisions. Besides his frustration over his inability to support his family in the United States, Martín also mentioned another factor that prompted him to return to Tlacuitapa instead of taking his family to the United States: the danger of clandestine border crossing. "I wouldn't take my family that way, endangering them to cross the border that way."

As Martín's case demonstrates, decisions to settle or return to Mexico are complex and are often based on noneconomic factors. While social networks can ease a migrant's transition to life in the United States by providing a home and access to job opportunities, other pressures such as separation from one's family, health issues, and quality of life may dissuade many migrants from remaining away from home.

SOCIAL SERVICES AND SETTLEMENT

The correlations between settlement in the United States and use of social services follow predictable patterns. The longer a migrant is based in the United States, the more likely he or she is to have children, to enroll them in public schools, to visit a doctor, or to become unemployed. The services that are most intimately tied to settlement in the United States are public education, health care, and unemployment compensation. Given that most migrants come to work in the United States when they are relatively young, it is highly likely that in succeeding years they will establish families and hold a succession of jobs in the United States. It is also evident that those who have children in the United States are more likely to settle where their children have access to a better opportunity structure. Having children in public school increases the likelihood that a migrant will settle in the United States. The use of other social services—such as welfare and food stamps—seems to be need-based and shows no significant relationship to settlement. Taking into account that settled migrants would have better access to information about the availability of these services, the lack of correlation between their use and settlement suggests that putting down roots in the United States may well increase the family's socioeconomic situation and reduce its need for social support.

Giving migrants access to social services is a hot-button political issue in the United States, particularly in areas where migrants tend to concentrate. Both Arizona and California have sponsored legislation to restrict undocumented migrants' access to non–federally mandated public benefits: Proposition 187 in California and Proposition 200 in Arizona. Three justifications drive the drafting of such legislation: (1) the perception that undocumented migrants draw from but do not contribute to public funds; (2) the belief that public benefits are a significant pull factor for migrants coming to the United States; and (3) the desire to send a message to the federal government that voters are dissatisfied with the enforcement of immigration laws (Ibarra 2004: 2; López 2004: 2; Díaz 2004: 2).

However, such legislation risks denying benefits to children born in the United States to immigrant families. These children are U.S. citizens who face distinct challenges. A lack of basic necessities, low socioeconomic status, and insufficient parental attention (due to migrants' exhausting work schedules) have been found to be significant factors in immigrant children's educational outcomes. "To compound these problems, families who have any members without full documentation feel the most vulnerable and therefore do not seek help from social agencies, even if they rightfully qualify to receive assistance" (Suárez-Orozco 1998: 258). According to one recent study, about three-fourths of all children of immigrants in the United States are native-born, and the majority of them live in mixed-status families (Fomby and Cherlin 2004: 586).

Education, Immigration, and Citizen Children

The education of migrants' children is one of the most important issues affecting settlement in the United States. We asked our interviewees about their own educational achievement, their level of English language proficiency, and whether their children were in school during their last stay in the United States—all factors that we hypothesized would influence settlement in the United States. We found that the migrants' level of education was relatively low. Of those who reported residing primarily in the United States, only 11.8 percent had completed the equivalent of a high school education. The number was slightly higher (12.9 percent) among documented migrants and substantially lower among undocumented migrants (6.1 percent). The modal level of educational attainment was completion of primary school (six years of education); 4.3 percent of respondents reported having a college degree.

The children of legal migrants are clearly benefiting from educational opportunities in the United States. However, U.S. school attendance by the children of undocumented migrants is much more limited (see table 5.3). Yet the majority of undocumented respondents with children in public school reported that their children were U.S. citizens. These migrant parents also reported that they paid taxes during their last stay in the United States, with all documented migrants and 89 percent of undocumented migrants with children in public school reporting that they had paid taxes (see table 5.4).

Table 5.3. Public Benefits Received During Most Recent Stay in the United States, by Immigration Status

	Undocumented Migrant (N = 180)	Legal Migrant (N = 119)	U.S. Citizen (N = 81)
Received medical attention at hospital[a]	44.7%	55.1%	60.0%
Received unemployment benefits[a]	6.7%	25.2%	34.6%
Received foodstamps[a]	3.4%	5.9%	8.6%
Received welfare benefits[a]	1.7%	4.2%	8.6%
Had children in public schools	9.0%	34.5%	42.1%

[a] Response also includes benefits received by family members whose immigration status could differ from respondent.

Table 5.4. Migrants Who Paid Taxes for Benefits Received in the United States

	Documented Migrants (N = 170)	Undocumented Migrants (N = 182)
Children in public school	100% of 64 cases	89% of 19 cases
Family receipt of medical attention	96% of 93 cases	74% of 82 cases
Unemployment	100% of 49 cases	86% of 14 cases
Food stamps	100% of 13 cases	4 of 6 cases
Welfare	100% of 11 cases	3 of 4 cases

Among the residents of Tlacuitapa and Las Ánimas, there is a correlation between place of principal residence and educational preference, with those who are based in Mexico more frequently reporting that they prefer their children to be educated in Mexico, and those based in the United States preferring a U.S. education for their children. Of those who live principally in Mexico, 48.2 percent prefer to educate their children in their home country, 39.3 percent in the United States, and the remainder in both countries. Of those who principally live in the United States, the difference is more pronounced, with 59.7 percent preferring to educate their children in the United States and 19.4 percent in Mexico, with the remainder preferring that their children be educated in both countries.

Health Care

As families become more established in the United States, they are more likely to use health care. Migrants whose primary residence remains in Mexico are less likely to use health services in the United States and often return to their place of origin in the event of an injury. This was the case for Benito, an agricultural worker who was injured picking oranges. Benito reported, "While picking oranges years ago, I fell and punctured my eye. I came back to Mexico to heal and not to bother the United States. I always pay for my own care, so I came to Mexico for the operation, to not bother the Untied States."

In our survey we asked respondents if they or any family member had received medical attention during their last stay in the United States and what method of payment was used to cover the cost. We also asked if the respondents had children born in the United States, but we did not ask specifically if the birth of their children or medical attention for their citizen children corresponded with their use of medical services. We found that 44.7 percent of undocumented migrants, 55.1 percent of documented migrants, and 60.0 percent of U.S. citizens reported having received medical attention in the United States for themselves or for a family member (see table 5.3).

Within our two research communities, we found that the costs of this use of health care in the United States were largely covered by the immigrants themselves, their insurance policies, and their employers' insurance polices. There are some interesting trends in health care use. Of the 194 interviewees who reported having received medical attention in the United States, 21.1 percent had their bills paid by Medi-Cal. In contrast, nearly 25 percent of respondents had paid their medical expenses out of pocket, 18.5 percent reported that their private health insurance covered the costs, and about 31 percent mentioned that their employers' insurance covered the expenses. Thus 74 percent of the medical care received by our respondents in the United States was paid for by the workers and their employers. Although these numbers demonstrate a high rate of self-payment, the fraction of respondents who reported having costs covered through their own private insurance is very low, suggesting a minimal level of health insurance coverage for the migrants and their families.

Looking at the cases of government-subsidized health care, the data indicate that most families who receive this benefit are of mixed legal status and are contributors to tax revenues. Ninety-six percent of documented migrants who reported that a family member had received medical attention also reported that they pay taxes, and 74 percent of undocumented migrants reported the same (see table 5.4). Among the forty-one interviewees who reported receiving Medi-Cal benefits, 38 percent were undocumented, and 100 percent of them reported that they contributed to the system through their taxes.

Cash Assistance

We found low utilization of cash assistance programs among migrants from the two research communities (see table 5.3). Of the nineteen recipients of cash assistance, four were undocumented and two of them have U.S. citizen children. Furthermore, all of the documented recipients and three-fourths of the undocumented recipients reported that they pay taxes (see table 5.4). Food assistance was also reported infrequently, numbering only twenty recipients; 3.4 percent of undocumented migrants and 5.9 percent of documented migrants reported that they or a family member received food stamps during their last stay in the United States. All documented migrants who received this benefit paid taxes, and the majority of undocumented migrants reported doing so as well. Considering that welfare benefits are among the few public benefits that can be legally denied to undocumented migrants, our study does not show that the "migrant drain" on such programs is significant, but it does confirm that over half of all families who receive these benefits have U.S. citizen children, who are legally entitled to receive such benefits.

Unemployment Compensation

Thirty percent of migrants settled in the United States reported that they had received unemployment benefits (see table 5.3). Because migrants who reside primarily in the United States are more likely to have extended work experience, they are also more likely to have been without work at some juncture. Of the sixty-nine respondents in our survey who reported receiving unemployment benefits, 23 percent were undocumented and about 28 percent had been injured on the job. Laborers in construction accounted for the highest percentage of recipients, with 30.1 percent of reported cases. The high risk of injury, the temporal nature of construction work, and the extreme winter conditions in the Tlacuitapeños' preferred destination (Oklahoma City) all help to explain the construction workers' more frequent receipt of unemployment benefits.

PROFILE OF MIGRANTS LIVING PRINCIPALLY IN THE UNITED STATES

Migrants currently settled in the United States share several characteristics that illustrate their integration into the fabric of American culture. However, there is a clear line that divides those settlers who are legally present and those who are not. While the majority of those currently settled in the United States are between 26 and 45 years of age, documented immigrants form an older population, with only 39 percent in the 26–45 age group, compared to 63 percent of undocumented migrants. Documented migrants based in the United States are also more likely to be married and have more children on average than is true for the younger and less experienced undocumented migrants. Many more documented than undocumented settled migrants are likely to have their nuclear families in the United States (see table 5.5). In terms of education, a majority in both groups has finished the equivalent of junior high school, and about 28 percent of both groups finished the equivalent of high school.

Documented and undocumented groups also display different patterns of settlement in the United States, with undocumented migrants relying more heavily on social networks. Documented migrants have much more experience living in the United States; 60 percent have been in the country between ten and thirty years, while the comparable number is 30 percent for undocumented migrants. Interestingly, our two research communities differ in terms of their preferred locations in the United States, with residents of Tlacuitapa being quite dispersed while those from Las Ánimas are grouped largely in California, principally in Los Angeles. However, small groups of migrants from Las Ánimas are establishing themselves in other places, such as Illinois and Oklahoma. And even though Oklahoma City has more Tlacuitapeños than does any other U.S. city, California is the state with the largest number of migrants from Tlacuitapa. Small groups of Tlacuitapa migrants have also established themselves in Illinois, Michigan, Nevada, New Jersey, Oregon, and Texas.

Table 5.5. Age and Family Structure of Migrants Residing in the United States

	Currently Settled Migrants	
Characteristics	Documented (N = 133)	Undocumented (N = 40)
Aged 26-45	39%	63%
Aged over 45	37%	10%
Married	68%	57%
Average number of children	2.2	1.3
Accompanied by spouse	70%	48%
Accompanied by children	65%	45%
10–30 years experience in the U.S.	60%	32%
Family networks influenced destination	77%	90%
Living with family or friends	39%	70%
Tlacuitapeño/Animeño neighborhood	15%	34%
Neighbors are of Mexican origin	12%	24%
Participates in social gathering of migrants in U.S.	46%	33%
Contact home once a week	33%	59%
Contact home twice a month	23%	23%
Contact home once a month	23%	8%
Visit home at least once a year	63%	37%
Visit home less than annually	23%	63%

The presence of relatives and friends was the most influential factor in the decision to settle in the United States for both documented and undocumented groups, although undocumented migrants are more dependent on these networks of friends and family. Nearly three-quarters of undocumented settlers were renting from or staying with family or friends during their most recent U.S. sojourn (see table 5.5). Undocumented migrants were also more likely to report having lived in neighborhoods where others from their hometown reside. Although fewer than half in either group participate in a social activity with others from their hometown or home country, documented migrants participate more often than do undocumented migrants. The most common activity shared by migrants in the United States is soccer, followed by church activities.

Undocumented migrants maintain more regular contact with their families in Mexico. However, migrants with papers more often report that their whole family lives in the United States, and they visit their hometown in Mexico more frequently than do undocumented migrants. Missing their relatives in Mexico was one of our interviewees' most frequent complaints about life in the United States, second only to the language barrier. Between 35 and 40 percent of both documented and undocumented migrants reported that they felt discriminated against in the United States at one time or another, yet discrimination was not mentioned as a leading complaint.

CONCLUSIONS

The movement of people out of our two research communities is a long-standing tradition, with generations of workers migrating, some returning and others making a new home in the United States. We hypothesized that border enforcement would have a significant impact on migrant settlement in the United States—specifically, that the increased danger and cost involved in crossing the border would discourage migrants from returning to their hometowns. There are numerous indications in our data that this is, indeed, occurring. Many of our undocumented interviewees have transferred their economic and family base to the United States, and some have done very well for themselves. Traces of their success can be seen in their well-built and maintained houses in Mexico, which now stand empty except when families return to their hometowns for vacation.

Once migrants arrive in the United States, they find that work is readily available. Fewer than 1 percent of migrants interviewed for our study reported that they were unable to find work during their most recent trip to the United States. Although it is commonly believed that undocumented workers find it harder to get jobs now than in the past, most of our interviewees continue to find jobs in an increasingly diverse array of industries.

Once a migrant is working in the United States, family reunification is one of the most significant factors influencing settlement. Leonor, a woman who has lived in California for over twenty years, confirms that the presence of the nuclear family in the United States can deter migrants from returning to Mexico permanently. When asked whether she would consider returning permanently to Tlacuitapa, Leonor answered, "I don't think so, because my roots are planted over there [in the United States]. Over there are my children, my grandchildren, and it is very difficult to leave the family. Maybe when we retire … we'll come for a longer time, but not to reside here."

Having U.S.-born children makes a migrant more likely to remain in the United States, especially if the children are of school age. Just as migrants prefer the economic opportunities in the United States to those in Mexico, they also prefer to educate their children in the United States, where they perceive a better opportunity structure for both education and employment upon completion of school. Although the migrants themselves have a low level of educational attainment, the importance they place on their children's education influences families to remain in the United States. Other factors that correlate with settlement in the United States are more likely the results of extended stays than causal factors. For example, any migrant family that has children in the United States will also need to tend to their medical care. Receipt of unemployment benefits is also significantly related to settlement, due to the extended periods that settled migrants spend in the U.S. labor market.

In the following chapter we look at the changing composition of the migrant flow from Tlacuitapa and Las Ánimas, which is beginning to include more women. Considering that returned migrants overwhelmingly reported that they had come home because they missed their families, the increased migration of women can contribute to a higher rate of settlement in the United States.

References

Chávez, Leo. 1992. *Shadowed Lives: Undocumented Immigrants in American Society*. Orlando, Fl.: Harcourt Brace College.

———. 1994. "The Power of the Imagined Community: The Settlement of Undocumented Mexicans and Central Americans in the United States," *American Anthropologist* 96, no. 1: 52–73.

Cornelius, Wayne. 1990. "Impacts of the 1986 U.S. Immigration Law on Emigration from Rural Mexican Sending Communities." In *Undocumented Migration to the United States: IRCA and the Experience of the 1980s*, ed. Frank Bean et al. Santa Monica, Calif.: Rand Corporation/Urban Institute.

———. 1992. "From Sojourners to Settlers: The Changing Profile of Mexican Migration to the United States." In *U.S.-Mexico Relations: Labor Market Interdependence*, ed. Jorge A. Bustamante, Clark W. Reynolds, and Raúl Hinojosa-Ojeda. Stanford, Calif.: Stanford University Press.

———. 1998. "The Structural Embeddedness of Demand for Mexican Immigrant Labor." In *Crossings: Mexican Immigration in Interdisciplinary Perspectives*, ed. Marcelo Suárez-Orozco. Cambridge, Mass.: David Rockefeller Center for Latin American Studies, Harvard University.

Díaz, Elvia. 2004. "Views from Both Sides of Prop. 200," *Arizona Republic*, September 19, http://www.azcentral.com, accessed November 3, 2004.

Fomby, Paula, and Andrew J. Cherlin. 2004. "Public Assistance Use among U.S.-Born Children of Immigrants," *International Migration Review.*

Ibarra, Ignacio. 2004. "Prop. 200's Potential Impacts Clear–As Mud," *Arizona Daily Star*, October 17, http://www.azstarnet.com/dailystar/printSN/438445.php, accessed October 20, 2004.

López, Steve. 2004. "Handouts? Go Beyond the Usual Scapegoats," *Los Angeles Times*, August 27, http://www.latimes.com/news/local/la-me-lopez27aug27,0,4604775.column?coll=la-headlines-california, accessed August 29, 2004.

Reyes, Belinda. 2004. "U.S. Immigration Policy and the Duration of Undocumented Trips." In *Crossing the Border: Research from the Mexican Migration Project*, ed. Jorge Durand and Douglas Massey. New York: Russell Sage Foundation.

Riosmena, Fernando. 2004. "Return versus Settlement among Undocumented Mexican Migrants, 1980 to 1996." In *Crossing the Border: Research from the Mexican Migration Project*, ed. Jorge Durand and Douglas Massey. New York: Russell Sage Foundation.

Suárez-Orozco, Marcelo M., ed. 1998. *Crossings: Mexican Immigration in Interdisciplinary Perspectives*. Cambridge, Mass.: David Rockefeller Center for Latin American Studies, Harvard University.

Torres Sarmiento, Socorro. 2002. *Making Ends Meet: Income-generating Strategies among Mexican Immigrants*. New York : LFB Scholarly Publishing.

6

Gender Differences

ELISABETH VALDEZ-SUITER, NANCY ROSAS-LÓPEZ, AND
NAYELI PAGAZA

> *I crossed in a car. I didn't have papers, and the coyote
> crossed me in the trunk of a car. It felt like despair... We
> were about six. The trunk was big and the air conditioning
> was on, but the darkness scared me. They were all women,
> and I paid about 3,000 dollars. We went to Los Angeles in
> the trunk.*—Dolores, a migrant now residing in Tlacuitapa.

Dolores's testimony reveals the harsh reality that many undocumented
female migrants endure when crossing into the United States. Over the
past two decades, women have begun migrating to the United States in
increasing numbers. This "feminization of migration" is partly a consequence of heightened border enforcement in the post-1993 period. As it
has become more difficult to cross the border without documents,
many male migrants are extending their stays in the United States or
traveling to their home country less frequently. Because they cannot go
home to see their wives and children, they are arranging for their families to join them in the United States (Donato and Patterson 2004: 111).

Although female migration is becoming more common, it is still
predominantly men who make the trip across the border. Hondagneu-
Sotelo (1994: 204) suggests that the historic reason behind this gender
bias is the bracero program, which recruited only male Mexican workers for agricultural labor in the United States. Bracero-era migration
created a pattern of behavior in which wives remained home with the
children while husbands sought temporary work in the United States.
The Immigration Reform and Control Act of 1986 (IRCA) likewise pro-

moted male entry by legalizing former undocumented migrants, the majority of whom were men (Donato and Patterson 2004: 114).

Mexican cultural norms have also played into the migration gender bias. Because women are perceived to be physically weaker than men, they are assumed to have a poorer chance of surviving the hardships of clandestine entry into United States. Further, Mexican women traditionally have not been expected to contribute financially to the household. Rather, their primary role is to care for the children and the home, leading many women to stay behind when their husbands journey to the United States. Wives who stay behind depend almost exclusively on the remittances their husbands send from the United States. According to Aysa and Massey (2004: 142), "as the quantity of monthly remittances increases, the odds that a wife works outside the home steadily decline, by about 4 percent for each additional hundred dollars received."

Until recently, female migration received only minimal attention among scholars. Regarding the treatment of women in the international migration literature, Shu-Ju Ada Cheng noted: "Women were either invisible or treated as dependents of male migrants without individual identities; the experiences, contributions and roles specific to their particular social locations were not distinguished conceptually from those of male migrants" (1999: 40). Although female migration is receiving more attention, there is still much to learn about this process and the characteristics that make women's migration experiences unique.

In this chapter we examine the sociodemographic profile of the female migrant, the motives that drive women to migrate (or to remain at home), women's modes of entry into the United States, and their situation once established there. Although more women are now migrating, we argue that their numbers are constrained relative to male migrants by their lower levels of education, employment, and income; higher reliance on family support; and higher perceived sense of danger in illegal border crossings.

RESEARCH METHODOLOGY AND GENDER BIAS

Twenty-seven percent of interviewees in our research communities were women, a proportion that reflects our particular survey methodology. Following our fieldwork protocol, interviewers surveyed male household heads first, followed by children (male or female) over the age of 14. If the male head of household was unavailable, the female head of household was interviewed about her husband's migration experience. Only if a female head of household volunteered that she had migration experience of her own was she interviewed on the basis of her own migration experience.

The fact that female heads of household were not interviewed by default, as were male household heads, led to a degree of gender bias in our interviewee population. For example, female respondents were younger on average, with over half between the ages of 15 and 24; male respondents had a more even age distribution (see figure 6.1). The most probable contributor to the gender difference in age distribution, aside from the possibility that more men between the ages of 15 and 24 were in the United States at the time of interview, is that the majority (64 percent) of the men interviewed were household heads, while the majority of female interviewees (66 percent) were daughters.

Figure 6.1. Age Distribution of Migrants, by Gender

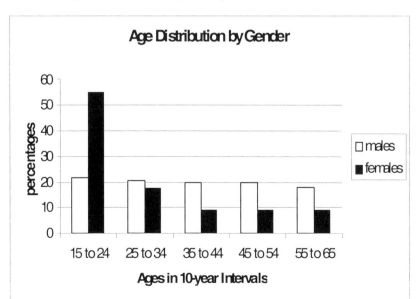

N = 603.

PROFILE OF THE FEMALE MIGRANT

One-quarter of the women interviewed in our survey had gone to the United States, compared to nearly three-fourths of the men surveyed. This gave a sample of forty female migrants. Their median age was 39, similar to the median age of 41 for male migrants. Both women and men who had *not* migrated to the United States were considerably younger, with a median age of 21 for nonmigrant women and 27.5 for nonmigrant men. Donato and Patterson (2004: 127) claim that "when women migrate without documents they do so at older ages." Given that we interviewed mostly young females (daughters), our sample may in fact underrepresent the number of women migrating to the United States. Our fieldwork protocol may have prevented us from reaching the older women who may be more likely to have migratory experience.

A hypothesis developed at the outset of the study was that women's relatively lower educational levels impeded their ability to migrate. In a traditional society, where men are expected to work and women remain at home, a family with limited resources may choose to invest in educating their sons rather than their daughters. Even if a family values education equally for their sons and daughters, educating a son is expected to bring a greater return given that men have a higher expected income, both at home and in the United States. Surprisingly, we did not find a significant difference between male and female migrants in their levels of formal education: more than half of both men and women said they had attended or completed elementary school. However, there was an educational difference between genders with respect to knowledge of English: 47 percent of female migrants claimed to understand some English, versus 57 percent of male migrants, whose English skills have clearly benefited from past migration experience (Alarcón 1989).

A lack of competence in English is a strong limitation on the type of job a person can obtain in the United States; jobs that do not require English usually pay low wages and have poor job security. Fear that their lack of English will prevent them from finding a well-paying job may explain why some potential first-time female migrants are hesitant about going to the United States. Their lack of English may also make them feel isolated and unsupported once they arrive there. In studying

Indian American motel owners, Nandini Narain Assar found that immigrant women typically had fewer language skills than immigrant men, and that women's lack of conversational English led to their greater isolation from society at large (Assar 1999: 89). It is easy to understand that the prospect of living in such relative social isolation might make migration unappealing to women.

Further, women have higher rates of unemployment in their home communities. When asked if they held a job in Mexico prior to their last trip to the United States, only 5 percent of female migrants said they were employed, compared to 33 percent of male migrants. In the 1980s, women in the Los Altos de Jalisco region were reported to be employed in a variety of jobs: from making, embroidering, and selling clothes out of their homes to driving trucks to transport cattle fodder (Hondagneu-Sotelo 1994: 13; Grindle 1988). During our field research, we found no evidence of women driving trucks or making clothing for sale. In Tlacuitapa, many women mentioned the local shoe factory as the *only* source of employment for women (see chapter 8). Some noted that the factory's wages were insufficient to support a family, and others mentioned abuse of employees as a reason to shun a job there. Yet despite their high rates of unemployment in their home communities, women do not cite the lack of job opportunities at home as a primary reason for migrating, perhaps because Mexican women traditionally have not been expected to contribute to the family's income.

MIGRATION HISTORY AND MOTIVES FOR MIGRATION

The median year of first migration to the United States for our female migrants was 1993, compared to a median first year of migration for men of 1983. The earlier onset of men's migration was expected given that men started migrating out of the region in the 1940s under the bracero program and that our male interviewees were older on average. Because male out-migration began earlier, it was also to be expected that male migrants average more trips to the United States than women (three versus two, respectively). Donato and Patterson support this finding: "on any given trip to the United States they [women] have less accumulated migratory experience than men" (2004: 127).

In addition, female migrants in our sample appear to be going to the United States for different reasons. Whereas men commonly state that they migrate out of economic necessity, female migrants were most likely to cite family reunification. One woman from Tlacuitapa mentioned that she had dreamed of visiting the United States since childhood, but only after she married did she make the journey—with her husband. She was apprehended by the Border Patrol on her first entry attempt and suffered cold and exhaustion on her second (successful) try. Despite the hardships, she remarked: "My happiest experience? Well I was with my husband. Of course it was sad, because I was leaving my family in Mexico, but I was with my husband."

While family reunification underpins most women's decision to migrate, some questions remain. Did women mention family reunification because they rely on family connections in the United States in order to make their journey? Will women who lack family support in the United States be less likely to migrate than men in the same situation? Of the male migrants in our sample who stated they did not have family in the United States, 36 percent had nevertheless traveled to the United States to work. However, not a single female migrant who had no family in the United States had migrated, suggesting that women are much more dependent on family support to make the journey.

Further evidence that female migrants rely more heavily on family ties is the greater percentage of women who receive financial support from family for their journey. Ninety-four percent of female migrants, versus only half of male migrants, had received financial support from family in Mexico or the United States for their most recent crossing to the United States (see table 6.1). It is almost impossible for women to self-finance their migration since, as noted, they are largely unemployed in Mexico and those who do work are poorly paid. It is not surprising, then, that more than a third of male migrants reported using their own savings to finance their trip, but only 6 percent of female migrants reported the same. Finally, whereas no female migrant received a loan from someone in her hometown to finance her trip, 12.2 percent of men had recourse to a local lender. This, too, may be attributable to women's lack of employment in the home community and the corresponding lack of loan collateral.

Table 6.1. How Migrants Collected Money to Pay for Most Recent Trip, by Gender

Source of Funds	Males	Females
Help from family already in United States	40.3%	68.8%
Help from family in Mexico	9.9%	25.0%
Personal savings	35.4%	6.3%
Loan from someone in hometown	12.2%	0.0%
Other	2.2%	0.0%
Total	100.0%	100.0%

$p = .019$; N = 197.

Women who migrate to reunite with family have the advantage of a preestablished social network. However, having family in the United States can be a mixed blessing. While a preestablished social network can help ease women migrants into life in the United States, families often discourage them from pursuing more independence there. Women migrants are at particular risk of being subjugated by their husbands, who may feel threatened by the freedoms and rights enjoyed by women in the United States. As migrant women gain employment in the receiving community and begin to contribute to household income, their influence within the family grows. Given the new opportunities open to them and their children, women migrants are more likely than men to want to remain in the United States (Hondagneu-Sotelo 1994: 100). Germán Vega Briones states that working in the United States has changed migrant women's perceptions about family and marriage practices. "In fact, for these women with international migratory experience, marriage is no longer the only option in life. Work and higher formal education begin to form part of their new life plans" (Vega Briones 2005). Because traditional Mexican men make the decisions in the family, they may feel threatened by their wage-earning wives and even send them home. María, a female migrant from Tlacuitapa who first migrated to the United States to reunite with her husband, explained:

> I believe that I would have been able to better myself
> there, but I came back because my husband wanted to
> come back.... He is from Tlacuitapa. Since he is from

> here, he would tell me, "Let's go, let's go." He came here
> first and I came later. I thought we were going to be here
> about two months and then would go back … come for a
> season only … but he didn't want to. That's not what
> happened. He would leave and I would stay here as a
> housewife.… I was always happy over there. I was never
> unhappy. I had all of the opportunities and help.

The reasons female nonmigrants give for remaining at home also shed light on the factors that drive women's migration. When nonmigrants in our study were asked if they planned to go to the United States in the coming year, there was no significant difference in responses between genders. For both, the majority of those who have not yet migrated do not appear to be planning to do so in the near future. However, the reasons given for not migrating differed (see table 6.2). Just as family ties are responsible for pulling the majority of female migrants to the United States, family ties are also likely to be keeping nonmigrant women at home. Casandra, a nonmigrant from Tlacuitapa, explained,

> I don't think of going north because, in a word, I am mar-
> ried. I have a family. But I am more worried about my
> mother's health. She is sick, and we have her under
> treatment. Then, well, I believe that I am going to stay
> here until the end.

Like women, men also gave a variety of reasons for not migrating to the United States, but topping the list was a lack of economic need. Many women also offered this explanation for not migrating, though more men than women seem to have a positive outlook regarding the possibility of "getting ahead" in Mexico without migration. Women were also less optimistic about the likelihood that an undocumented Mexican could find work in the United States: 64 percent of women, compared to 47 percent of men, thought that it is currently very difficult to get a job without papers. This relative pessimism among women may be another factor deterring women from migrating in the first place. The second-most-common response by nonmigrant men—that they were too old to migrate—reflects our survey methodology. If we had included more older women in our survey, it is possible that this response would have emerged more frequently among nonmigrating women as well.

Table 6.2. Why Some Respondents Were *Not* Planning to Migrate 2005, by Gender

Reasons Given for Not Migrating	Males	Females
No economic necessity	16.2%	14.3%
Sees possibility for advancement in Mexico without migrating	6.7%	2.2%
More difficult to cross without papers now than before	13.4%	17.6%
Lack of money to pay for *coyote*, transport	5.0%	3.3%
Doesn't like fast-paced life of United States	4.5%	3.3%
Family difficulties	8.9%	22.0%
Has family, friends in Mexico: "Everyone knows me"	1.7%	4.4%
Illness (own)	7.3%	2.2%
Age: too old	12.3%	1.1%
Age: too young	3.9%	5.5%
Not interested	7.8%	11.0%
Has to finish studies	2.2%	5.5%
Other	10.1%	7.7%
Total	100.0%	100.0%

$p = .005$, N = 270.

Notably, the second-most-common reason cited by *both* sexes for not migrating was the increasing difficulty of border crossing. The Border Patrol's stepped-up presence is thus playing strongly in the decisions of both male and female nonmigrants. However, stronger border enforcement appears to be affecting women more: 17.6 percent of women, versus 14.3 percent of men, mentioned the difficulty of crossing the border as their top reason for not migrating. And when analyzing the responses of all interviewees in our survey (migrants and nonmigrants), a significantly higher percentage of women (91 percent) believed that crossing into the United States without legal documents is

very dangerous, versus 81 percent among men. This heightened perception of danger may be influencing women's method of entry into the
United States, as will be discussed below.

METHODS OF ENTRY AND BORDER-CROSSING EXPERIENCE

The most notable difference between male and female migrants regarding methods of entry is whether they had legal documents the first time
they came to the United States. Over half of the female migrants in our
survey had crossed with legal documents on their first trip, compared
to only 20 percent of the men (see table 6.3).[1] This difference reflects the
high percentage of women who migrate for family reunification pur-
poses. In many instances, the husband has already acquired immigration papers for his wife, allowing her to cross legally on her first trip.[2]

Table 6.3. Method of First Crossing, by Gender

Method	Males	Females
With no documents (or with falsified documents)	79.8%	43.8%
With documents	20.2%	56.3%
Total	100.0%	100.0%

$p < .001$; N = 289.

However, the fact that women have a heightened sense of the risks
involved in clandestine border crossing may also be playing into the
difference found in terms of documentation status. It is possible that
women's perceptions of danger prompt them to wait for documents or
to not cross at all rather than cross illegally.

Common wisdom holds that women will have a harder time over-
coming the physical challenges of a clandestine border crossing and will

---

[1] For the most recent crossing, we see the same trend. Sixty-five percent of females, compared to 46 percent of males, crossed with papers on their most
recent trip.

[2] According to Donato and Patterson (2004: 114), "Mexican women are much
less likely than men to migrate independently, and their moves are strongly
linked to relatives already living north of the border."

also face higher risks of sexual and physical assault than men. Ramón, a migrant from Tlacuitapa, was asked how he would feel about his wife crossing the border alone:

> One fears the worst. As her husband I had to cross with her precisely because one never knows how many women are abused. I only went for her protection, because I didn't need to cross [illegally].

Despite these perceptions, we found no evidence that female migrants actually experience more hardship or danger than male migrants. Considering only the migrants who had crossed the border illegally, we found no significant difference between men and women's judgment as to whether the crossing was more or less difficult than expected. Likewise, there was no significant difference between genders regarding any physical harm or discomfort experienced while crossing the border, nor was there any significant difference regarding rates of apprehension by the Border Patrol. This last finding contrasts with Donato and Patterson's study, which found an average apprehension rate of 13 percent for undocumented women, compared to 29 percent for men (2004: 118).

Although women, like men, endure many hardships when crossing the border, some seem to manage this undertaking with ease. Diana, who crossed through a U.S. port of entry hidden in a car, said of her experience: "I never regretted it. I thought it was easy the first time. I never had trouble. I would do it again. With everything I know, I would still go." Women like Diana who have migrated at least once often express a willingness to migrate again, while those who have never migrated express anxiety about attempting it for the first time. In short, women's fear of migrating appears to be based more on a fear of the unknown or of the worst-case scenario than on a previous bad experience. It is also interesting to note that women are more fearful of crossing the border illegally even though men appear to be more aware of the dangers of crossing. Forty-five percent of men mentioned hearing about the dangers of border crossing on television; the comparable figure among women was only 28 percent. Furthermore, among all respondents, more men than women knew about recent Border Patrol efforts to increase enforcement at particular points of entry (75 percent of men, versus 65 percent of women). One reason that men are more likely to know about these enforcement efforts is their own migratory experience.

Finally, it may be that women are more fearful of crossing the border clandestinely because they are more likely to be crossing with their children. Sixty-one percent of female migrants in our study reported having their children with them in the United States during their most recent stay, versus only 36 percent of the men surveyed. Yet female migrants were no more likely than men to have crossed the border along with their children. This leads us to conclude that the children reported to have been with their migrant mothers during recent stays were likely born in the United States. This finding is confirmed by the numbers: considering only migrants who have children, 62 percent of female migrants, but only 40 percent of male migrants, have children born in the United States. This may explain why female migrants are more likely than men to stay long term in the United States (Cornelius 1990). These women want their children to benefit from the opportunities available to them as U.S. citizens, and they do not want to run the risk of returning home for a visit only to find that they cannot return with their citizen children. Ana, a migrant from Tlacuitapa who was pregnant when she crossed the border, explained, "My baby was born in the United States. I believe that his future is better over there than here.... He has more security and his future is better than his brothers.'"

ONCE IN THE UNITED STATES

Because family ties largely determine whether a woman will stay in her home community or migrate, we would expect female migrants in the United States to maintain closer contact than male migrants with family members in the sending community. Although we found no significant difference between male and female migrants with regard to the frequency of visits home, we did find that women migrants contact their relatives in Mexico more frequently: 57 percent of women, versus 37 percent of men, said they call home at least once a week.

Some female migrants who no longer have immediate family in Mexico still feel a strong obligation to help extended family members and even neighbors in their home communities. Cinthia is a naturalized U.S. citizen who, along with her husband and three U.S.-born children, has made Las Vegas her home for more than fifteen years. Despite being well established in the United States, Cinthia tries to visit Tlacuitapa every year. "I come during the Christmas festivities, and I bring clothes that don't fit my sons anymore for the sons of my neighbors. I try to help my people however I can."

Women's strong ties to family in Mexico are also reflected in the money they send to their families. The amounts and frequency of remittances did not differ significantly between female and male migrants. However, women make less money in the United States (a median monthly salary of $952 versus $1,400 for male migrants on most recent trip), so they are sending a higher percentage of their income home.

Women migrants earn the money they remit to Mexico working in a variety of occupations in the United States. Of course, women are more likely than men to support their families by caring for the home and children in the United States, while men are significantly more likely to hold wage-earning jobs in the United States (table 6.4). Almost all male migrants in our sample held wage-earning jobs during their last stay in the United States. This is particularly impressive when considering that the latest figures reported 5.2 percent unemployment for the entire male population in the United States and 6.4 percent unemployment for Latino men (Bureau of Labor Statistics 2005). One-fifth (21 percent) of female migrants in our sample did not hold a wage-earning job during the most recent stay in the United States.

Table 6.4. Percentage of Paid/Unpaid Work among Migrants, by Gender

Type of Work	Males	Females	Total
Paid	99.4%	79.1%	97%
Unpaid or worker retired/ disabled	0.6%	20.9%	3%
Total	100.0%	100.0%	100%

$p < .001$; N = 347.

Even though female migrants are less likely to be gainfully employed, they are working in a variety of occupations in the United
States, many of which are far removed from the kinds of work they
might do in Mexico. Table 6.5 summarizes the types of work in which
wage-earning migrants engage in the United States. During their most
recent stay in the United States, nearly half of male migrants worked in
construction, followed by agriculture and livestock raising, gardening
and landscaping, and the restaurant industry. For female migrants, the
most popular employment sector was manufacturing or factory work,
followed by restaurant work. Tying for third place was construction, an
occupation that is practically unheard of for women in Mexico. While a
man in Mexico might feel threatened or embarrassed if his wife worked
in construction, we spoke to many migrants who were open-minded
concerning a woman's ability to work in a variety of occupations. Tlacuitapan migrant Luis, speaking about his wife, explained: "[In the
United States] it is not important what she does; they don't notice
women working in construction. Over there it is normal." Aysa and
Massey argue that the mere fact that women are entering the workforce
is also likely to "increase their power and bargaining position in the
family" (2004: 142).

Table 6.5. Type of Employment of Wage-Earning Migrants, by Gender

Employment Type	Males	Females
Agriculture/livestock raising	11.20%	2.90%
Construction	47.80%	11.80%
Childcare or eldercare	0.90%	11.80%
Factory work	5.60%	26.50%
Gardening/landscape	9.30%	0.00%
Cleaning houses, buildings	2.80%	8.80%
Restaurant work	8.70%	17.60%
Social/public services	2.50%	2.90%
Store clerk/stocker	1.20%	8.80%
Other	9.90%	0.80%
Total	100.00%	100.00%

$p < .001$; N = 356.

Due in large part to women's lower likelihood of having a wage-paying job in the United States, we found that fewer women pay taxes on income. Although there is no significant gender difference when it comes to filing tax returns, 46 percent of female migrants, versus 65 percent of male migrants, reported that income taxes were deducted from their wages. In addition to the fact that fewer women are earning an income, women are also more likely to be employed in the informal sector, where taxes are not automatically deducted from paychecks. Hondagneu-Sotelo found a tendency for female migrants to work in jobs that are "informally organized, unregulated, untaxed and unre-corded remunerated services" (2001: 239). The significant percentage of women working in childcare/eldercare and housecleaning underscores this trend (see table 6.5).

Women who do not hold wage-earning jobs are less likely to receive health care. When we asked migrants who had paid for medical attention in the United States the last time such attention was needed, 12 percent of male migrants but only 3 percent of female migrants reported covering the costs themselves. The fact that men are more likely to pay for their own health care can be attributed in part to the fact that men receive higher average wages than employed women. Men are also more likely to receive medical insurance through their employer; 15 percent of men versus 4 percent of women reported that insurance provided by their employer had paid for their family's medical services. If a woman needs medical attention, the costs of care are most likely to be covered by her husband or her husband's insurance. Women's extreme dependence on men when medical attention is required is an overlooked danger associated with the female migrant experience in the United States.

Women's reliance on male family members in the United States is exacerbated by the fact that women also seem to have less access to social networks outside the home. When asked if they participate in any social groups when in the United States, 35 percent of men versus only 19 percent of women responded in the affirmative. Women are most likely to participate in church-related social groups (50 percent), while men are most likely to participate through sports (45 percent). In Mexico, social pressure essentially compels women to attend Mass and to be involved in religious activities, while men are encouraged to play soccer and be physically active on weekends. These traditions seem to both help and hurt women in the United States. Though the tradition of church involvement supports some female migrants in their search for a social outlet in their new community, the tradition of women's exclusion from sports is preventing them from participating in another common (and healthy) social outlet.

CONCLUSIONS

Although female out-migration from Tlacuitapa and Las Ánimas is increasing, just as it has increased across Mexico in past decades, women still face many challenges that depress their propensity to go north. Women have fewer opportunities to migrate due to lower levels of education, employment, and income in their home community. They are less likely to understand English, which can severely limit their job prospects and social networks if they decide to go to the United States. Women were also more pessimistic about their ability to find work in the United States, a belief that, in and of itself, could be deterring many women from migrating. Higher unemployment rates and low wages in Mexico do not allow women to accumulate funds to pay for their trip, leaving them more dependent on family for financial assistance when migrating. Lower levels of paid employment and lower wages in the United States may also be serious obstacles to women's ability to receive medical attention, given that they are less likely to have insurance or to be able to pay out of pocket for such care.

More women than men are crossing legally into the United States, a finding strongly linked to women's higher likelihood of relocating for family reunification. Women are also more likely to have U.S.-born children, which increases the likelihood that they will want to stay longer in the United States. Thus, while men are migrating primarily to find work, female migrants are establishing deeper roots through family and legal residence in the United States. Nevertheless, this trend is symptomatic of female migrants' greater reliance on family, illustrated by the fact that not a single female respondent had migrated without having some family member already established in the United States.

Women who lack such a family network appear to have no alternative but to remain in the home community.

Women expressed fear of crossing the border illegally, even though we found no evidence that they were actually suffering more than men in their attempts to enter the United States, neither in terms of injuries nor in apprehension rates. Men were also more informed about recent efforts to strengthen border enforcement and were more likely to have heard about the dangers of crossing illegally. Perhaps knowing what the real dangers are, no matter how severe, is less frightening than are imagined dangers.

One result of great interest was the fact that many women in our research communities mentioned loneliness as a key reason for their desire to migrate. The elderly women of Tlacuitapa have watched their town change over the years. They have seen young men—and, increasingly, young women—leave for the United States. Every year they have watched these young migrants return for the annual fiestas and then leave again once the festivities have ended. One town resident described Tlacuitapa during those times of the year: "The town is completely empty and alone, because all the people leave … and every year another bunch leaves, and every year a bunch of young women get married and their husbands take them with them. Nobody stays."

References

Alarcón, Rafael. 1989. "Gracias a Dios y al Norte: Tlacuitapa, Jalisco, y su relación con los Estados Unidos." Manuscript. La Jolla: Center for U.S.-Mexican Studies, University of California, San Diego.

Assar, Nandini Narain. 1999. "Immigration Policy, Cultural Norms, and Gender Relations among Indian-American Motel Owners." In *Gender and Immigration*, ed. Gregory A. Kelson and Debra L. DeLaet. New York: New York University Press.

Aysa, Maria, and Douglas S. Massey. 2004. "Wives Left Behind: The Labor Market Behavior of Women in Migrant Communities." In *Crossing the Border: Research from the Mexican Migration Project*, ed. Jorge Durand and Douglas S. Massey. New York: Russell Sage Foundation.

Bureau of Labor Statistics. 2005. "Employment Situation Summary." Washington, D.C.: U.S. Department of Labor, May 6, http://www.bls.gov/news.release/empsit.nr0.htm.

Cheng, Shu-Ju Ada. 1999. "Labor Migration and International Sexual Division of Labor: A Feminist Perspective." In *Gender and Immigration*, ed. Gregory A. Kelson and Debra L. DeLaet. New York: New York University Press.

Cornelius, Wayne A. 1990. "Impacts of the 1986 U.S. Immigration Law on Emigration from Rural Mexican Sending Communities." In *Undocumented Migration to the United States: IRCA and the Experience of the 1980s*, ed. Frank D. Bean et al. Santa Monica, Calif. and Washington, D.C.: RAND Corporation/Urban Institute.

Donato, Katherine M., and Evelyn Patterson. 2004. "Women and Men on the Move: Undocumented Border Crossing." In *Crossing the Border: Research from the Mexican Migration Project*, ed. Jorge Durand and Douglas S. Massey. New York: Russell Sage Foundation.

Grindle, Merilee S. 1988. *Searching for Rural Development: Labor Migration and Employment in Mexico*. Ithaca, N.Y.: Cornell University Press.

Hondagneu-Sotelo, Pierrette. 1994. *Gendered Transitions: Mexican Experiences of Immigration*. Berkeley: University of California Press.

———. 2001. *Doméstica: Immigrant Workers Cleaning and Caring in the Shadows of Affluence*. Berkeley: University of California Press.

Vega Briones, Germán. 2005. "El estudio de la migración internacional desde una perspectiva de género: el caso de Ciudad Juárez, Chihuahua." Presented at the seminar "Mujeres y Migración en las Fronteras de México," organized by the Instituto Nacional de Migración, March 8.

7

Migration and Generational Cohorts

Luz María Henríquez, Monica Cornejo, and Sofía Aguilar

> *The older ones leave for the United States, and the young peo-*
> *ple see them return with a new car or new clothes, all dressed*
> *up. And they think, "wow, it only took them a couple of years,*
> *Wow, I want to go, too."*—Marcos, 38-year-old migrant
> from Tlacuitapa and president of a labor union in Union
> City, California.

Four generations of men and women from Tlacuitapa and Las Ánimas have left to work in the United States, becoming part of a deeply embedded culture of migration in their home communities. Although many patterns and characteristics of migration have remained constant over the years, the profiles and experiences of migrants from these communities have also come to differ in certain respects, depending on when a migrant made his or her first journey to the north. In this chapter we explore these differences across generations with respect to migrants' personal characteristics, border-crossing experiences, occupations, and opinions on various migration-related issues.

In order to facilitate comparison, we grouped migrants from our 2005 survey into four cohorts based on the year the migrant first entered the United States: bracero program–era migrants (1900–1964),[1] post–bracero program migrants (1965–1985), Immigration Reform and Control Act of 1986 (IRCA) migrants (1986–1992), and new border enforcement migrants (1993–present) (see table 7.1). We selected the cohorts on the basis of

---

[1] The bracero program began in August 1942, following an exchange of diplomatic notes between the United States and Mexico. We use this program as the denominator for this cohort because it was the most notable influence on Mexico-to-U.S. migration up to the mid-1960s.

specific U.S. migration policies that we hypothesized would affect the migration experience of each group. The chapter begins with a brief description of the policies relevant to each cohort, followed by an exploration of the changes that have occurred in migrant profiles and experiences by generation. By looking at each cohort independently and in relation to the others, we aim to determine the extent to which migration patterns have changed over time and the degree to which U.S. immigration policies have or have not affected the culture of migration existing in our research communities.

Table 7.1. Migrants, by Generational Cohort

Migrant Cohort	As Percent of Total Migrant Population
Bracero era	4.8%
Post–bracero era	47.6%
IRCA era	15.3%
New border enforcement era	32.3%
Total	100.0%

N = 353.

U.S. IMMIGRATION POLICIES BY COHORT

The Bracero Program Era, 1900–1964

The "bracero" program was a contract labor program created in 1942 by the U.S. and Mexican governments in response to the World War II–induced shortage of labor in the U.S. agricultural industry. The program allowed independent farm associations and the Farm Bureau to bring Mexican peasants to the United States to work in agriculture under contracts that specified the period for which the "bracero "could work, after which he was required to return to Mexico.

The bracero program was officially terminated in 1964, although the U.S. Congress had begun to limit the program as early as 1961 by, for example, not allowing braceros to use power-driven machinery nor to participate in canning and packing activities. Mounting protests by U.S. labor unions over violations of labor standards by employers using bracero labor ultimately sealed the program's demise.

The Post–Bracero Program Era, 1965–1985

After the bracero program ended, the U.S. Congress passed several laws that restricted the number of Mexican migrants allowed into the United States in any given year. A law passed in 1963 required employers who hired immigrant workers and sponsored their petitions for permanent residency visas to obtain a certificate indicating that qualified U.S. workers were not available to perform the job for which immigrants were being sought (Calavita 1992: 147). Because employers were previously allowed to sponsor up to twenty-four workers for permanent visas without a labor certification, the new law made it much more difficult for farmers to employ Mexican migrants legally.

The IRCA Era, 1986–1992

The Immigration Reform and Control Act of 1986 was designed to control illegal immigration into the United States by punishing employers who knowingly hired undocumented workers, increasing spending on border enforcement, and legalizing certain classes of undocumented immigrants. IRCA's "amnesty" component allowed immigrants who had been living illegally in the United States before January 1982 to apply for legal status by May 1988. The legislation also included a special legalization program for migrants who could prove a history of agricultural employment in the United States. Once an immigrant legalized under IRCA, he could then apply for legal admission to the United States for close family members. Many migrants from our research communities eagerly seized this opportunity to reunite their families on the U.S. side of the border. Alfonso, a resident of Tlacuitapa, described the emotional costs immigrants bear when leaving their dependents:

> Earning money makes me happy, but I have to leave the family here in Tlacuitapa. So you are like half an orange, and you need to bring your family to the United States and live together there in order to complete the orange.

Given that families naturally want to reunite, the IRCA amnesty programs led to an increased incidence of whole-family migration to the United States from our research communities. In the two years immediately following the passage of IRCA, numerous dependents of "amnestied" household heads followed them to the United States, whether or not the dependents themselves could qualify for legalization under IRCA and years before the household head could petition for their admission as permanent legal residents (see Cornelius 1989).

The New Border Enforcement Era, 1993–Present

The generation of migrants that began to cross into the United States for the first time in 1993 has been exposed to strong anti-immigration sentiments and restrictive policies in the United States. Following a wave of xenophobia, Californians passed Proposition 187 in 1994, which sought to deny social services, including health care and public education, to undocumented immigrants. This legislation, which was later declared unconstitutional, played upon the fears of many California residents that "illegals" were a drain on the state's economy and public services. Beginning in 1993, the administration of President Bill Clinton began implementing programs to tighten border control in key corridors for illegal entry. Concentrated border enforcement operations like "Hold the Line" in Texas and "Gatekeeper" in California sought to reduce the flow of illegal immigrants entering the United States by deterring migration at its sources in Mexico.

SURVEY RESULTS

Our survey of Tlacuitapa and Las Ánimas residents having U.S. migration experience revealed a number of similarities and differences among the four migrant cohorts. Although most of the differences reflect the specific migration experiences of each cohort, there are also differences across the generations due simply to differences in median age. Migrants who crossed into the United States for the first time during the bracero era are obviously older, on average, than the generation of migrants who first crossed the border during the recent period of enhanced border enforcement. The first two topics discussed below—agriculture as a livelihood and education—are directly linked to this age difference between cohorts. Although these topics may not have a direct relationship with each cohort's specific border-crossing history, they nevertheless provide for a better understanding of each cohort's demographic profile. The remainder of the chapter deals with issues that relate more directly to each cohort's migration experience—namely, legal status, border-crossing experience, U.S. destination, and occupation while in the United States.

Agriculture as Livelihood

Although agriculture has long been the leading economic activity in both Tlacuitapa and Las Ánimas, it has lost prominence in recent years and is definitely waning in appeal among the younger generation. The shift away from agriculture is by no means limited to our research communities; Mexico's small-scale agricultural producers are finding it increasingly difficult to make a living, due in great part to increased competition from the United States since the implementation of the North American Free Trade Agreement (NAFTA) in 1994. As a result, small producers across rural Mexico are seeking economic options outside of agriculture.

Lacking access to reliable banking institutions where they could safeguard their money, rural Mexicans have traditionally "stored" their wealth in land or livestock. It is likely that older generations of migrants invested the money they earned in the United States in these agricultural assets. Our findings support this: not only do bracero-era migrants own more cattle than do migrants from more recent generations, they also own more land compared to more recent migrants (see tables 7.2 and 7.3).

Table 7.2. Cattle Ownership, by Migrant Cohort

Migrant Cohort	Percent Who Own Cattle	Percent Who Do Not Own Cattle	Total
Bracero era	47.1%	52.9%	100%
Post–bracero era	24.4%	75.6%	100%
IRCA era	11.3%	88.7%	100%
New border enforcement era	9.0%	91.0%	100%

N = 349; $p < .0001$.

Because agriculture has become less profitable, migrants are now somewhat reluctant to invest their U.S. earnings in land or cattle. They are choosing, rather, to invest in home construction in Mexico, homes purchased in the United States, or other nonagricultural assets. The new trucks and new homes that are proliferating in Tlacuitapa and Las Ánimas are examples of the investments that migrants are making with their U.S.-earned income. The shift out of agriculture as a primary or even secondary source of income can only be expected to increase in our research communities, unless significant structural changes are implemented to make Mexico's agricultural sector more profitable.

Table 7.3. Land Ownership, by Migrant Cohort

Migrant Cohort	Percent Who Own Land	Percent Who Do Not Own Land	Total
Bracero era	75.0%	25.0%	100%
Post–bracero era	36.3%	63.7%	100%
IRCA era	28.0%	72.0%	100%
New border enforcement era	9.3%	90.7%	100%

N = 331, $p < .0001$.

Education

The varying levels of education among our migrant cohorts largely reflect the educational opportunities available to migrants in their hometowns during childhood. Tlacuitapa's primary school has been operating since 1958, and the secondary school, since 1967. Given that the latter was established after the bracero period ended, we found a much lower level of secondary education among the bracero-era cohort: the majority of bracero-era migrants reported completing some or all of primary school (70.6 percent), but relatively few had completed secondary school (see table 7.4).

We expected, and found, a notable jump in secondary school attendance among the post-bracero cohort, which reflects the opening of the secondary school. What is more difficult to explain, however, is why secondary school attendance dropped for migrants in the IRCA cohort. It may be that migrants from this cohort opted out of secondary education in order to take advantage of job opportunities in the United States.

Finally, the new border enforcement cohort as a whole exhibited the most years of secondary and high school education relative to other groups, and a relatively high level of university education as well. The educational pattern in rural Mexico is for children to attend school longer than did their parents. Given that migrants in the most recent cohort are expected to be younger, it is logical that they would have higher education levels on average, as our results suggest.

Legal Status

A migrant's legal immigration status on his or her first border crossing differed significantly across the four cohorts, due in part to the different U.S. immigration policies in effect during each period. Three-quarters of bracero-era migrants crossed with legal documents the first time they entered the United States (see table 7.5). This is to be expected; as participants in the bracero program, they crossed the border with their temporary work permits. The fact that one-fourth of bracero-era migrants crossed without documents indicates that not everyone in this cohort sought a "bracero" contract, or was able to obtain one. Rubén, an octogenarian from Tlacuitapa, told us that his father opted to work in the mines in Utah rather than in agriculture through the bracero program.

The significant drop in documented migration between the bracero and post-bracero generations was a direct result of the termination of the bracero program and the implementation of a number of U.S. policies to restrict the number of legal Mexican migrants entering the United States (Durand, Massey, and Parrado 1999). Surprisingly, we did not see a major increase in the number of migrants entering the United States with legal documents during the IRCA period, something that one might have expected given the legalization programs implemented during that period. We may, however, be seeing a delayed effect of IRCA's amnesty provisions in the increase in the proportion of documented entries among migrants in our new border enforcement cohort. That is, their higher numbers for entries with immigration documents may reflect policies implemented during the IRCA period. This could occur, for example, if the applications that migrants filed under IRCA to obtain legal status for family members in Mexico were not processed or approved until the mid-1990s.

Table 7.4. Education Level, by Migrant Cohort

Migrant Cohort	None	Primary School (grades 1–6)	Secondary School (grades 7–9)	Preparatory School (grades 10–12)	University	Total
Bracero era	0%	70.6%	5.9%	5.9%	—*	100%
Post–bracero era	10.7%	54.8%	28.4%	3.6%	3.6%	100%
IRCA era	3.7%	70.4%	16.7%	5.6%	3.7%	100%
New border enforcement era	5.3%	48.7%	29.2%	9.7%	7.2%	100%

N = 352, p = .014. * = insufficient cases.

Table 7.5. Legal Immigration Status by Migrant Cohort
(on first trip to United States)

Migrant Cohort	Percent Who Entered without Documents	Percent Who Entered with Documents	Total
Bracero era	75.0%	25.0%	100%
Post–bracero era	15.30%	84.70%	100%
IRCA era	17.40%	82.60%	100%
New border enforcement era	31.30%	68.70%	100%

N = 292, $p < .0001$.

Border-Crossing Experiences

U.S. immigration policies obviously shape the difficulties and dangers that migrants encounter when attempting to cross into the United States, and the trend in immigration policy over our four immigration periods has been toward stronger border enforcement. This is reflected to some degree in our interviewees' judgments of the difficulty they experienced when crossing the border without documents (table 7.6). All undocumented migrants from the bracero cohort indicated that they had no difficulty crossing the border the first time they migrated to the United States. During the bracero period, there were few agents patrolling the border and few physical barriers to clandestine entry. This changed drastically in post-bracero years. Nearly two-thirds of our undocumented migrants from the post–bracero era cohort indicated that they encountered some difficulty their first time crossing the border. Moreover, although the U.S. Immigration and Naturalization Service did not have adequate funding to function effectively during this period, it nevertheless gave "the impression of a substantial increase of officer personnel" (Calavita 1992: 150).

In our next two cohorts we find a moderate but continuous decrease in the perceived difficulty of border crossing, despite rising U.S. investments in border enforcement. This can be explained in large part by factors that eased would-be immigrants' first border crossing. Primary among these was the gradual development of transborder social networks. Family members and friends already established in the United

States provided, and continue to provide, guidance and advice to first-time crossers. In our three most recent cohorts, at least 80 percent of the migrants reported having family members in the United States prior to their first migration (table 7.7). These social networks were often initiated by pioneer migrants who went to the United States in the bracero era—men who were generally the first members of their families to go north. The fact that 100 percent of IRCA migrants reported having relatives in the United States prior to their first migration illustrates the strong shift toward family reunification migration that occurred during that period.

Table 7.6. Perceived Difficulty of Border Crossing, by Migrant Cohort Generation (first trip to United States)

Migrant Cohort	Percent Who Found Crossing Not Difficult	Percent Who Found Crossing Somewhat/ Very Difficult	Total
Bracero era	100.0%	0.0%	100%
Post–bracero era	34.4%	65.6%	100%
IRCA era	40.0%	60.0%	100%
New border enforcement era	47.0%	53.0%	100%

N = 230; p = .03.

Table 7.7. Social Networks in the United States, by Migrant Cohort (first trip to United States)

Migrant Cohort	Percent with Relatives in U.S.	Percent with No Relatives in U.S.	Total
Bracero era	43.8%	56.3%	100%
Post–bracero era	83.2%	16.8%	100%
IRCA era	100.0%	0.0%	100%
New border enforcement era	92.0%	8.0%	100%

N = 350; p < .0001.

Interestingly, the new border enforcement cohort reported encountering less difficulty when crossing into the United States than did migrants from the post-bracero and IRCA periods (see table 7.6). This result may reflect another change, which, like social networks, has functioned to facilitate migrants' entry: increased reliance on *coyotes* to bring migrants across the border, a topic discussed in detail in chapter 4 of this volume.

U.S. Destination

California has been the most popular U.S. destination for all four of our migrant cohorts on their first entry into the United States, and this state accounts for 100 percent of bracero-era migrants (see table 7.8). This finding is particularly surprising given that El Paso, Texas, was the largest recruitment and registration site for the bracero program. Moreover, Texas is geographically closer to our research communities than is California, which led us to expect that most of our bracero-era migrants would have worked in Texas on their first trip to the United States. It may be that these braceros went to California not by choice but because that is where they were contracted to work. Bracero contracts were presented in English, and migrants often signed the contracts without fully understanding their rights or the conditions of their employment (Marentes and Marentes 1999).

Following the bracero period, subsequent cohorts migrated in lesser numbers to California and increasingly to Oklahoma, Oregon, and Illinois. Similar, though less notable, increases have occurred across generations in migration to the states of Texas, Nevada, Michigan, Florida, and Arizona. The emergence of these new destinations is partly a function of the shift in migrants' U.S. employment, away from the agricultural sector and toward construction and services, as discussed below. The move away from California and toward other states with shorter histories of Mexican immigration may also be explained by migrants' search for labor markets that are less saturated with immigrants than is California's.

Migrants' Occupations in the United States

The majority (82.4 percent) of bracero-era migrants from our research communities worked in agriculture during their first trip to the United States (table 7.9), a finding that reflects these migrants' strong participation in the agricultural contract labor program. Although many continued to work in agriculture following the end of the bracero program in 1964, the drop-off in agricultural employment between the bracero and

Table 7.8. U.S. Destination, by Migrant Cohort

Migrant Cohort	California	Oklahoma	Oregon	Illinois	Other
Bracero era	100.0%	0.0%	0.0%	0.0%	0.0%
Post–bracero era	66.7%	7.7%	0.0%	2.6%	23.0%
IRCA era	50.0%	11.4%	4.5%	6.8%	27.3%
New border enforcement era	56.5%	14.1%	7.1%	4.7%	17.6%

N = 329; p = .886.

Table 7.9. Sector of First Employment in the United States, by Migrant Cohort

Migrant Cohort	Agriculture	Construction	Services	Manufacturing	Retail	Professional	Other	Total
Bracero era	82.4%	17.6%	0.0%	0.0%	0.0%	0.0%	0.0%	100.0%
Post–bracero era	33.1%	17.5%	30.0%	12.5%	0.6%	0.0%	6.3%	100.0%
IRCA era	5.9%	29.4%	54.9%	3.9%	2.0%	0.0%	3.9%	100.0%
New border enforcement era	10.1%	49.5%	24.2%	7.1%	4.0%	3.0%	2.0%	100.0%

N = 327; p < .0001.

post-bracero periods is notable, with only a third of the post-bracero cohort working in agriculture during their first stay in the United States. Some migrants may have started looking for employment outside of agriculture because of the harsh working conditions and treatment that they endured under the bracero program. Tlacuitapa resident Marcos recalled his father's experience as a bracero in the United States: "They treated them like animals, putting them in big warehouses and spraying them down, just like animals, to clean them up, rid them of any disease, and put them in the field."

While employment in the agricultural sector has declined across cohorts, employment in construction and services has increased. Looking at the most recent generation of migrants, the largest share (49.5 percent) work in construction, while nearly a quarter work in the service sector and only one-tenth work in agriculture. The surge in migration to Oklahoma is linked to the recent increase in construction jobs in that state. It is interesting to note that new border enforcement–era migrants are the first cohort to report any employment as professionals. Since professional jobs typically require a good understanding of English, this finding may reflect the overall higher education level of this most recent migrant cohort.

CONCLUSION

Analyzing our survey data by generation has allowed us to more deeply explore the culture of migration that has evolved over time in our research communities. There has been a general shift away from agriculture in Mexico in recent years, and later generations of migrants are much less likely to invest their U.S. earnings in cattle and land than were earlier generations of migrants. Our results also revealed differences among migrant generations in terms of education, influenced in large part by the educational facilities that were available to each cohort. The fact that the most recent cohort has a higher education level overall suggests that its members might be able to take better-paying, higher-skilled jobs in the United States—jobs that previous cohorts of migrants were not qualified to fill.

With respect to border-crossing experiences, we found that undocumented bracero-era migrants crossed into the United States with relative ease and that subsequent migrant cohorts had greater difficulty crossing the border without papers. Nevertheless, IRCA migrants reported less difficulty than post–bracero era migrants, and the new border enforcement–era migrants reported even less difficulty, indicating the importance of social networks in the United States and border crossers' greater reliance on *coyotes* to evade the Border Patrol. Finally, we found an overall occupational shift across cohorts away from agriculture and toward employment in construction and services, a change that is directly linked to a destination shift away from California and toward Oklahoma, Illinois, Oregon, and other U.S. states.

Whereas migrants from the bracero period were predominantly farmworkers, the most recent cohort of migrants comprises cooks, construction workers, landscapers, caregivers, and even professionals. These most recent migrants clearly have moved up the occupational ladder, but their ability to do so has been conditioned by the pioneering efforts, hard work, and networks put in place by the migrants who preceded them. As future generations of migrants enter the United States, their experiences and opportunities will likewise be shaped by the migrants who came before them, and the culture of migration will continue to evolve.

References

Calavita, Kitty. 1992. *Inside the State: The Bracero Program, Immigration, and the I.N.S.* New York: Routledge.

Cornelius, Wayne A. 1989. "Impacts of the 1986 U.S. Immigration Law on Emigration from Rural Mexican Sending Communities," *Population and Development Review* 15, no. 4: 689–705.

Durand, Jorge, Douglas S. Massey, and Emilio A. Parrado. 1999. "The New Era of Mexican Migration to the United States," *Journal of American History* 86, no. 2.

Marentes, Carlos, and Cynthis P. Marentes. 1999. "The Bracero Project," http://www.farmworkers.org/bracerop.html, accessed June 8, 2005.

8

Migration and Local Development

BRISELLA CANTÚ, FAWAD SHAIQ, AND ANJANETTE URDANIVIA

> *Economically, our situation is very bad.... On the one hand,*
> *we are well off [in terms of remittances], but on the other*
> *hand, we don't have any sources of work. Without sources*
> *of work, there is no wealth.... This town will become deso-*
> *late if new sources of work do not arise; that's the main rea-*
> *son that people leave in the first place.*—Raúl, a 56-year-old
> experienced migrant from Tlacuitapa.

Tlacuitapeños and Animeños migrate to the United States for a variety
of reasons (see chapter 3), most of which are economic in nature. This
chapter examines in detail how the local economies of Tlacuitapa and
Las Ánimas have shaped migration to the United States and how migration, in turn, has affected the course of development in these towns.
We begin by exploring how real and perceived deficiencies in the local
economic opportunity structure of these communities are influencing
out-migration. This discussion includes an assessment of the impacts of
a recently established factory that produces athletic shoes in Tlacuitapa,
as well as an analysis of local residents' perceptions of the impacts of
the North American Free Trade Agreement (NAFTA) on their local
economy. We also present a general profile of the characteristics that
prompt migrants to send varying amounts of remittances back home,
and we analyze the impacts of these remittances on the economies of
our research communities. Finally, given that the development effects
of migration are sociocultural as well as economic, we discuss how
residents perceive migration to be affecting their cultural traditions and
moral values.

LOCAL OPPORTUNITY STRUCTURE

It is generally recognized that migration to the United States from rural Mexico is driven by a combination of "Mexico-push" and "U.S.-pull" factors. To gauge the relative importance of these factors, we asked our interviewees in Tlacuitapa and Las Ánimas: "Did you go to the U.S. [most recently] mainly because of the conditions in Mexico, or because of the opportunities available in the U.S.?" A large majority (82 percent) replied that they went north to take advantage of opportunities available in the United States. However, our respondents were also sensitive to "push" factors in their hometowns. We posed the following question: "Some people say that a young person who was born here in Tlacuitapa/Las Ánimas can succeed in life without leaving the town; other people say that to succeed, a young person has to leave to the U.S. What do you think?" Seventy-two percent of our interviewees chose the latter alternative, indicating their belief that a young person cannot progress by staying in their hometown. This belief is grounded in an accurate perception of local labor markets.

Employment

Tlacuitapa and Las Ánimas offer very little in terms of employment opportunities, especially outside of the declining agricultural sector. For many residents, such as Raúl, who is quoted at the beginning of this chapter, finding a job in the United States is the only viable option for economic mobility. When our interviewees were asked what they thought it would take for fewer people to migrate from their hometowns, over 90 percent mentioned some type of employment-related change (figure 8.1). In a 1995 survey of Tlacuitapa (Cornelius 1998), when respondents were asked the same question, the proportion who cited job-related solutions was equally high (92.4 percent).

Among our interviewees, the need for more and better-quality jobs substantially outweighed other considerations, such as educational opportunities, better governance, and infrastructure development. These results suggest that, while government programs that aim to slow out-migration by improving rural infrastructure are important, they are unlikely to be effective without simultaneous efforts to expand and diversify the employment base in sending communities.

Figure 8.1. What Would Be Necessary for Fewer People to Leave This Town?

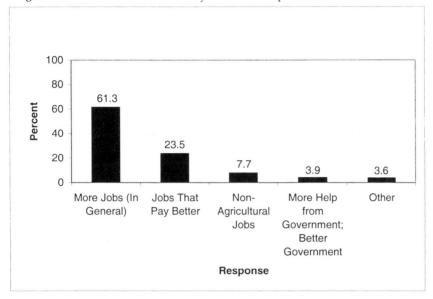

N = 587.

Perceptions of the Local Opportunity Structure

Numerous items in our questionnaire dealt with the opportunities that people *perceived* were available to them. We would expect people with more positive perceptions of their local opportunity structure to be less likely to migrate. However, our data indicate that this is not the case; people with positive perceptions of the local opportunity structure and those with negative perceptions both migrate to the United States in equally large numbers. The fact that people with positive perceptions of the local opportunity structure are migrating at a rate comparable to that of people holding negative perceptions suggests that many are being pulled by more lucrative job opportunities available in the United States. Our analysis likewise found no difference between experienced migrants and nonmigrants in terms of their views of the local opportunity structure; a majority of both groups believed that one must leave the hometown in order to succeed in life.

Although the majority of respondents had negative perceptions of the local opportunity structure in their town, 79.9 percent believed that migration to the United States had benefited the local economy. David Fitzgerald (2005) asked the same question in the migrant-sending town of Arandas, Jalisco. Fitzgerald's results mirrored our own, with roughly three-quarters of respondents believing that migration had benefited Arandas economically. What most people seem to mean by this is that the remittances (to be discussed later in this chapter) that migrants send back to their towns have helped keep the local economies afloat. Yet, despite remittances' undeniable economic benefits for migrant-sending communities in Mexico, there are many negatives associated with them as well: making recipients dependent on this source of money, encouraging more migration among people who otherwise could form a local workforce, and decreasing the probability of governmental and/or private investments. Citing these and other concerns, approximately one-fifth of our respondents expressed the belief that migration had hurt their town's economy. Nevertheless, people who view migration as harmful to their hometown's economy migrate in numbers proportional to those who believe that migration has helped their town economically.

To understand the propensity to migrate, it is important to consider not only how people perceive their living conditions at present, but how they believe their quality of life might change in the future. We asked our interviewees to rate their family's present living conditions on a scale from 1 to 10, and then we asked them whether they thought their families would be living better, worse, or the same in five years' time. We found that people who rated themselves higher on the first scale were more likely to be planning to migrate to the United States in the next twelve months. In fact, people who rated themselves at the highest levels (scores of 9 or 10) were significantly more likely to migrate to the United States than were individuals who ranked themselves lower. Similarly, when asked about their economic situation within the next five years, the more optimistic the respondent, the more likely he or she was to be planning to migrate to the United States during the next twelve months. These results indicate that people who intend to go north are more positive about their future prospects, no doubt because they are sanguine about the opportunities awaiting them in the United States.

Tlacuitapa's Shoe Factory

Prior to the opening of an athletic shoe factory in Tlacuitapa in 2004, there were very few nonagricultural employment opportunities available to residents of the community. As of January 2005, the factory employed roughly fifty-five of the town's younger residents, overwhelmingly women. Sonia, a 19-year-old employee of the factory, commented,

> Before this factory came to Tlacuitapa, there was nothing here for us women.… We had to rely on whatever our parents would provide for us. At least now we have some financial freedom.

Sonia's words echo the sentiments of most of the factory's employees whom we interviewed, who also saw the factory as a partial solution to the town's employment problem. However, despite being one of the few businesses with job openings in a town suffering from an anemic employment base, the shoe factory cannot maintain a stable workforce. A large percentage of its employees leave for the United States every year. This section discusses the dynamics of the shoe factory's operations and attempts to explain why its employees continue to go north.

Both the state and local governments worked to bring the shoe factory to Tlacuitapa. The municipal government offered rent-free occupancy of a former CONASUPO warehouse, and local *ejidatarios* provided rent-free land. As a result, the factory owners pay no property taxes, only taxes on the sale of their products. Government support was especially visible in the initial months of the factory's operations. When the factory opened, its owners needed to pay only for the machines, the light fixtures, and tables; all other operating capital was supplied by the government. In addition, the government provided training subsidies for the factory's new workers.

According to the factory manager, 80 percent of his workers are female. Most are single, young (between 13 and 30 years of age), and, on average, have completed seven years of schooling. To attract potential employees, the factory uses a state subsidy of 450 pesos a week for the first month of training and work. A typical day for a worker begins at 8:00 am and ends at 5:30 pm, and includes a half-hour lunch break and two short bathroom breaks. Workdays are Monday through Friday, and the factory is also open on Saturdays for employees wishing to earn extra money. The factory is set up as an assembly line, with each employee assigned a particular task to ensure that production runs efficiently. The newer employees rotate to different tasks to decrease the monotony of the work and to increase productivity by expanding everyone's job skills.

After the initial month, the entry-level base salary is between 50 and 60 pesos a day. These wages are relatively high compared to Jalisco's minimum wage of 44.05 pesos per day in January 2005. The factory manager stated that employees are paid for each quota of sixty pairs of shoes that they complete. Employees also receive benefits based on seniority and skill level. As employees learn more skills and hone the ones they already possess, they are able to move up the company ladder and increase their salaries further.

Despite these salaries, worker turnover remains quite high. Employees reported that 60 percent of workers left within a year, while the factory manager claimed a much lower, though still significant, annual turnover rate of 25 percent. The manager said that most of this turnover was due to employees who migrated to the United States to earn higher wages. In fact, on the day when we interviewed the factory manager, four employees had quit, citing their intention to go north. Another factor in the high turnover rate may be the unwillingness of some of the town's young women to take jobs at the factory because of unfavorable working conditions.

The shoe factory's manager worked previously at the company's headquarters in San Francisco, Guanajuato State, but he decided to open the Tlacuitapa plant in order to compete for other markets in Mexico. He explained:

> If my warehouse [in San Francisco] was producing 1,200 pairs a week, the industry was asking for 1,200 a day.... We could not keep up with demand solely with our factories in San Francisco, because it was a highly competitive area and we were competing for workers with numerous industries. I was one of the executives situated in

the San Francisco plant and proposed to the owner that
we needed to establish factories in small towns that lack
the competition of other industries and have large numbers of unemployed residents. This was the only way we
could compete and become successful. It would take
some financial investment on our part, but in this com-
petitive industry it was the only way to succeed.

The manager chose Tlacuitapa as the site for his new factory because of the town's pool of available workers. While the factory contin-
ues to train new employees, these workers can leave the factory for the
United States at any time. The manager noted that, despite opening the
Tlacuitapa factory, the company's factories cannot produce enough
shoes to meet demand. As of January 2005, the Tlacuitapa factory was
producing about 600 pairs of shoes a day, using 55 employees. The
manager had plans to expand operations into a second warehouse in
Tlacuitapa, hoping to employ 200 workers by the end of 2005. To expand the workforce and to replace workers who leave for the United
States, the manager said that the factory would begin recruiting workers from nearby smaller localities where, he believed, the residents have
greater economic need.

The challenge of retaining these workers will be huge. Although the
average salary paid to the shoe factory's workers exceeds Jalisco's
minimum wage, it cannot begin to compete with the wages a migrant
can earn in the United States. Martha, a 19-year-old unmarried factory
worker who makes just enough money to get by, told of a neighbor's
daughter who earns enough in Oklahoma City to support both her
family in Oklahoma and her parents in Tlacuitapa at a relatively high
standard of living. She will undoubtedly feel the pull to migrate north
as well.

Impacts of NAFTA

On January 1, 1994, the implementation of the North American Free
Trade Agreement established a trade bloc comprising Mexico, Canada,
and the United States, in which import tariffs were drastically reduced
or completely eliminated. Supporters predicted that NAFTA would

sharply reduce the gap in living standards between Mexico and the United States, but this has not occurred. Cheap U.S. agricultural imports flooded Mexican markets, driving Mexican prices and wages down. Because of the U.S. government's farm subsidies, U.S. growers were able to sell their corn in Mexico at 30 percent or more below the cost of production between 1999 and 2002 (Institute for Agriculture and Trade Policy 2003). Meanwhile, prices paid to Mexican corn farmers dropped by 70 percent (Bureau of Citizenship 2003). Mexican agriculture has been a net loser in trade with the United States, and employment in the agricultural sector has declined sharply. As U.S. exports of subsidized crops have depressed agricultural prices in Mexico, the rural poor have borne the brunt of economic liberalization, and they have been forced to do so without adequate government support (Polaski 2004).

This blow to Mexico's agricultural sector has increased migration out of rural areas to the country's already overcrowded cities, where high underemployment rates are further depressing wages, and it is spurring more international migration as well. The surge in U.S.-bound migration among rural Mexicans is a direct result of the fact that small Mexican farmers have been unfairly forced to compete with U.S. government–subsidized factory farms. Marcos, a 38-year-old Tlacuitapeño living in Union City, California, put it this way:

> Most of the farm people left Mexico because of the government's commitment to free trade, to NAFTA.... Nobody does any agricultural work anymore, nobody, because it's not worth it, it's just not worth it.... It's the same with corn. If we grow and sell corn, we used to get good money for it, but not anymore. It's cheaper to buy corn than investing all the hard work to grow it ... all the money for fertilizer, seeds, this and that, not counting all the hours you put into it yourself. You see all the fields just sitting there, growing weeds. I think NAFTA deeply affected all the farmworkers here. And that's why everybody is migrating over there.

Marcos's negative views of NAFTA were echoed by most of his neighbors. When we asked our interviewees whether NAFTA had been harmful or beneficial, 60 percent said that the trade agreement had hurt them. The most common complaint was that prices for agricultural products had dropped while the costs of agricultural inputs had risen, making it impossible for rural Mexicans to compete with cheaper U.S.-grown products.

Agricultural production was already a precarious undertaking in Tlacuitapa and Las Ánimas. Under the additional burden of NAFTA's deleterious impacts, these towns' agricultural sectors are faring even worse; 41.8 percent of our respondents claimed that prices for agricultural products are so low that farmers cannot make a living. One farmer explained how working the fields essentially means working for free:

> The crops that the farmers produce are no longer worth growing, products like corn…. The fertilizers are just too expensive and … what is produced is sold at a very low price. People no longer want to pay … and if you calculate everything, the labor comes out to be free.

Even if these small farmers are overstating NAFTA's verifiable impacts on agricultural prices, the outcome is the same. As long as rural Mexicans view their economic situation as being dragged down by NAFTA and without solution, they will continue to migrate to the United States.

REMITTANCES IN THE LOCAL ECONOMY

Migrants to the United States typically remit large portions of their earnings back to dependents who have remained in Mexico. The largely positive view that our interviewees hold of migration's economic impacts on their home communities is due to the consistent inflow of these remittances. Remittances are often a lifeline for migrants' families, and, when given collectively, they fund infrastructure improvements in sending communities. The total amount of Mexican migrants' remittances in 2005 was estimated at more than US$20 billion, exceeding the foreign direct investment that Mexico received that year as well as revenues from tourism.

The economies of labor-exporting communities like Tlacuitapa and Las Ánimas are heavily dependent on remittances for their survival. This section looks at various aspects of remittances, at both the sending and the receiving end: What factors make it more likely that a migrant will send money, and what factors determine how much is sent? How are remittances being used, and could they be invested more effectively to promote productive, job-creating development?

Remittance-Sending Behavior

The majority of migrants from Tlacuitapa and Las Ánimas (71.7 percent) reported that they had remitted money to their families during their most recent stay in the United States. The most important factor influencing how much money a migrant will remit to his or her hometown is the salary that the migrant earns in the United States. Our migrant interviewees' median monthly salary during their most recent sojourn in the United States was $1,400, and the median monthly amount remitted to Mexico was $300. We found a significant positive correlation between income level and amount remitted, up to an income threshold of $2,000 per month. When we analyze remittances as a percentage of a migrant's pay, the positive correlation holds up to an income threshold of $1,600 per month (see table 8.1, figure 8.2).

The fact that remittances initially rise as a percentage of earnings is consistent with the primary reason that Mexicans migrate to the United States: to work to support their families. Given that their families' well-being is their top priority, migrants have minimal incentive to improve their own standard of living in the United States even if they receive a higher salary. According to our results, migrants in the United States subsist on a semi-static budget, so that any budget surplus that accrues through higher wages tends to be remitted to the family in Mexico.

Table 8.1. Remittances as a Percentage of Salary Earned in the United States

Migrant's Salary (in U.S. dollars)	$300– $800	$801– $,1200	$1,201– $1,600	$1,601– $1,800	$1,801 and up
Average remittance as percent of salary	21.6%	27.3%	32.9%	22.6%	23.9%

N = 204.

Figure 8.2. Remittances as a Percent of Migrant's U.S. Salary

N = 204.

One possible explanation for the drop in the absolute and proportional amounts of remittances among migrants earning higher salaries is that these migrants have been in the United States for a longer period of time and thus may already have brought their nuclear families to the United States as well. Further analysis of our data confirms that migrants who leave their families in Mexico send significantly more in remittances compared to migrants whose families are with them in the United States.[1] Once a migrant's immediate family joins him or her in the United States, it can be assumed that the family is on the path toward settlement. According to one recent study of remittance behavior by Lowell and de la Garza (2002), for every one percent increase in time spent in the United States, the likelihood of remitting decreases by 2 percent. Consistent with this result, Lowell and de la Garza found that migrants who have permanent legal resident ("green card") status are

---

[1] Nevertheless, even migrants whose families are with them in the United States send considerable amounts of money to extended family members and even neighbors in their home community.

more likely to remit than are naturalized U.S. citizens, who are more likely to have the majority of their family in the United States.

Another indicator of migrants' ties to Mexico is the frequency with which they contact their family in their home community. Our data reveal a significant relationship between the level of an immigrant's contact with family in Mexico and the amount of money remitted home. While just under a fifth of migrants who contact their families only once a month send $500 per month or more to family in Mexico, nearly one-third of those who contact their families every week send that amount (table 8.2)

Table 8.2. Remittances in Relation to Degree of Contact with Family in Mexico

Level of Contact	Remittance Amount (U.S. dollars)			
	$1–$250	$251–$500	$501–$750	$751 and up
Once a week	29.9%	38.5%	5.1%	26.5%
Once every two weeks	45.1%	31.4%	13.7%	9.8%
Once a month	58.7%	21.7%	6.5%	13.0%

N = 214; *p* = .003.

Use of Remittances and Local Development

To understand the impacts that remittances have on the local economy of a migrant-sending community, we must examine how that money is spent by the families that receive this income. The vast majority of families (83 percent) in our research communities use remittances primarily for food and general household maintenance. If we consider medicine and health care as general household maintenance as well, the percentage jumps to 89 percent (figure 8.3). San Román, a 16-year-old Tlacuitapeño who has never migrated to the United States, observed:

> Remittances are great. People send money, and it helps out the town; this is the main reason the town has survived for so long. Although the town is obviously a bit neglected, it is still up and running. The people are poor, but they still live a middle-class lifestyle. They have their small cars, and the money even suffices to buy gas and tires. Before, they didn't even have money for beans and tortillas, but now they are in a better economic situation.

Figure 8.3. Primary Use of Remittances

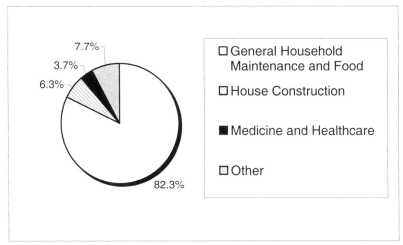

7.7%
3.7%
6.3%
82.3%

☐ General Household
   Maintenance and Food

☐ House Construction

■ Medicine and Healthcare

☐ Other

N = 271.

While fewer people mentioned house construction or improvement, this was another common purpose to which townspeople directed the remittances they received. A visitor to these communities can view this investment in the proliferation of two-story and sometimes three-story U.S.-style cement homes. Laura, a 24-year-old Tlacuitapeña, explained: "People earn a lot more money over there, and because of that we have nice homes, nice trucks, and overall a better life for our kids." The fact that health care was commonly mentioned as a use for remittances underscores the failure of Mexico's health system to provide affordable health care to its citizens.

In addition to providing money that families use for basic household maintenance, remittances can serve as an engine for economic development in migrant-sending communities—*if* they lead to local job creation. The most visible link between remittances and job creation in our research communities is the construction of new homes financed with money sent home by migrants. Ana, a 36-year-old single mother in Tlacuitapa, described how "money earned in the United States goes to construct homes here in Tlacuitapa, which generates more work." Although the creation of these construction jobs can be viewed positively, these are temporary jobs. Once a house has been built, the workers become unemployed once again, and they will remain so until the next migrant decides to build his or her dream house.

There is a wide gap between the kind of development that can create sustainable, long-term employment and this stop-and-go employment, which has no prospect of becoming a sizable and integral part of the local economy. Channeling remittances into permanent job-creating enterprises is the only way that remittances can curb the flow of U.S.-bound migrants from communities like Tlacuitapa and Las Ánimas.

CULTURAL IMPACTS OF MIGRATION

The act of migrating from a small rural town to a foreign country, and often to a big city in that foreign country, can fundamentally change migrants' attitudes about their local customs and values. Given the long-standing tradition of out-migration from Tlacuitapa and Las Ánimas, the majority of these towns' residents have been exposed to new ideas, morals, and values, either directly, by living as migrants in the United States, or indirectly, through contact with return migrants who bring new cultural ideas home with them. This section discusses the views that people from our research communities hold regarding the ways in which migration has shaped their towns' culture and values.

Although our informants hold a generally positive view of migration in terms of its economic impacts in their communities, more than half of those surveyed believed that migration had negatively affected their towns' customs and values (figure 8.4). Carmen, the owner of the local arcade in Tlacuitapa, complained, "Values have been lost and forgotten.... People move away and forget about our culture and the fundamental things in life; they tend to forget where they come from." Carmen's sentiments are shared by residents in towns across Mexico that are characterized by long traditions of emigration. In Arandas, Jalisco, for example, Fitzgerald (2005) found that approximately three-fourths of the town's residents felt that migration had exerted negative impacts on their town's customs and moral values.[2]

---

[2] Whereas our 2005 survey in Tlacuitapa and Las Ánimas allowed respondents to answer that migration had "benefited a town's cultural and moral values in

Figure 8.4. Has Migration to the United States Benefited or Harmed This Town's Customs and Moral Values?

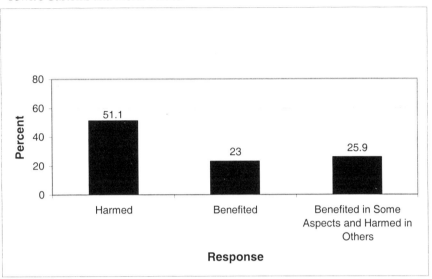

N = 557.

When asked exactly how local customs and values had been compromised, more than a third (37 percent) of our interviewees cited the "negative attitudes" of the younger generation, followed by drug use (table 8.3). Older residents in particular see the younger generation as too "liberal" in their attitudes and behavior. They worry especially about the decline in moral values of their town's young women. Herminia, a middle-aged married woman from Tlacuitapa, believes that

> Tijuana and the United States have become the ruin of most girls. When I was a young girl, my parents would never let me go to the plaza. But nowadays, it's two or three in the morning and girls are out in the garden, talking to their boyfriends ... acting as if it was okay.

some aspects and harmed it in other aspects," Fitzgerald's survey required respondents to identify which had been stronger, the positive or the negative impacts. This difference might account for Fitzgerald's report of a higher percentage of respondents with negative views.

Table 8.3. Ways in Which Migration to U.S. Undermines Community Values

Responses	Percent
Young peoples' negative attitude	36.7%
Drug usage	32.1%
Traditions/customs/celebrations have lost their meaning	25.7%
Religion is no longer practiced	3.7%
Other	1.8%
Total	100.0%

N = 109.

Martha, an older woman from Tlacuitapa who attends Mass every Sunday, commented: "The priest here hates the new morality, especially women studying and such." Concepción, who has two young sons, sees a major difference in how young girls today deport themselves: "They no longer have any morals nor any care for their reputation." Interviewees like Herminia, Martha, and Concepción sense that their traditions and values are under attack because they are no longer respected nor adhered to by the younger generation. Migration has led to the injection of a healthy dose of feminism into conservative Tlacuitapa and Las Ánimas. However, it is clear that not all in the community, including its leaders, are ready to accept it.

Our respondents also expressed concern that migration has led to increased drug use in their communities. Nearly a third of people who felt that migration had generated negative impacts cited drugs as the principal problem. An elderly woman commented in the local general store that "the younger boys join the older boys who are up to no good;... the young ones are so inexperienced that they do not know what drug addiction is." María, another Tlacuitapa resident, similarly believed that "too many young people are arriving with drug addictions. They use drugs ... they plant marijuana and get cocaine from friends who come from the United States."

We have no hard evidence that drug use in Tlacuitapa and Las Ánimas is as prevalent as many residents believe. Nevertheless, such is the level of concern that there may very likely be some drug activity in the community that was not present before. Nonmigrant families in particular were concerned that their sons would be lured to drugs by the young migrants who return to the community each year for the annual fiestas. These young migrants, who return with new clothes, new cars, and new ideas, are often idolized by nonmigrating young people. If these migrants are using drugs, it is no surprise that parents worry that their children will mimic these *hijos ausentes* and use drugs as well.

One-quarter of the people who held a negative view of migration's impacts on customs and values believed that migration was leading to a loss in traditions, such as retaining close family ties and knowing one's history and culture. Return migrants bring social and cultural ideas that are very different from those of nonmigrating townspeople. Adolfo, a middle-aged Animeño, lamented that "the new generation has forgotten about their principles and morals; they have opted instead to live an American way of life." The migrants who live and work in the United States are exposed to many new ideas and behaviors. "They know more than those who decide to stay" (Levitt 1998: 930), and when they return to their communities of origin they are often seen as outsiders because of this newly acquired knowledge.

A final, less frequently mentioned reason that respondents offered for the perceived cultural meltdown of their communities is a decrease in religiosity. As discussed in chapter 2, Tlacuitapa and Las Ánimas are very conservative and very religious towns. Religion is a moral framework, a compilation of beliefs, and a sense of personal identity for many people in these communities. The church is the focal point of the town, as in most rural towns across Mexico. While church leaders might disapprove of the ideas and values that migrants bring home with them, they are also eager to foster good relations with these migrants, given that they represent a huge potential source of funds that the church can use to better its position within the town.

CONCLUSION

Our data reveal that migration is being driven by a combination of local economic conditions (push factors) and opportunities that lure prospective and returning migrants to the United States (pull factors). Trade liberalization has exacerbated out-migration from rural areas to the United States as fewer people are able to support their families through farming. However, emigration is such a deeply entrenched behavior in these communities that even people who see a positive local opportunity structure still migrate. Migration's embeddedness is confirmed by the case of the shoe factory in Tlacuitapa, which, despite offering relatively high wages, loses many of its employees to migration because of the even higher wages in the United States. Our respondents associate migration with a prosperous future, basing their class status and their families' future prospects on the opportunity to migrate.

Migrants' remittances provide essential help to those who remain behind. Residents of our research communities use remittances to purchase food and other household necessities, as well as to build and improve houses and obtain medical care. Although most of our respondents view the economic effects of migration in a positive light, there is also a widespread sense that migration is leading to a decline in cultural traditions and a corruption of moral values.

Emigration has provided Tlacuitapa and Las Ánimas with a vital lifeline. Remittances are providing crucial support for the local economies; without the constant influx of dollars from the north, it is likely that the economies would collapse and these communities would soon be ghost towns. The crucial challenge is determining how remittances can be channeled more effectively into the creation of more and better jobs that might allow more would-be migrants to remain at home.

References

Bureau of Citizenship and Immigration Services. Office of Policy and Planning. 2003. "Estimates of the Unauthorized Immigrant Population Residing in the United States, 1990 to 2000."

Cornelius, Wayne A. 1998. "Ejido Reform: Stimulus or Alternative to Migration?" In *The Transformation of Rural Mexico*, ed. Wayne A. Cornelius and David Myhre. La Jolla, Calif.: Center for U.S.-Mexican Studies, University of California, San Diego.

Fitzgerald, David. 2005. "Emigration's Challenge to the 'Nation Church': Mexican Catholic Emigration Policies, 1920–2004." PhD dissertation, University of California, Los Angeles.

Institute for Agriculture and Trade Policy. 2003. "United States Dumping on World Agricultural Markets." Cancun Series, Paper No. 1. Minneapolis, Minn.: Institute for Agriculture and Trade Policy.

Levitt, Peggy. 1998. "Social Remittances: Migration-Driven Local-Level Forms of Cultural Diffusion," *International Migration Review* 32: 926–48.

Lowell, Briant Lindsay, and Rodolfo O. de la Garza. 2002. "A New Phase in the Story of Remittances." In *Sending Money Home*, ed. Rodolfo O. de la Garza and Briant Lindsay Lowell. New York: Rowman and Littlefield.

Polaski, Sandra. 2004. "Mexican Employment, Productivity and Income a Decade after NAFTA." Paper submitted to the Standing Senate Committee on Foreign Affairs, Canada, February 25.

9

Migration and Political Involvement

WILLIAM CHIU AND MARISOL RAQUEL GUTIÉRREZ

> *Little has changed since President Vicente Fox came to power. One presidential term is not enough to judge. Some people are not satisfied with Fox; the people are very divided. I was not able to vote in 2000, but if possible I would like to vote in 2006 from the United States. We want Mexico to be a better country.*—José, a 56-year-old experienced migrant who resides in Tlacuitapa.

Mexican migrants abroad can and do play politically influential roles in their communities and countries of origin.[1] The Mexican diaspora is seeking active inclusion in Mexico's political affairs by demanding the vote abroad and by pursuing citizenship rights abroad as well. Migrants' participation in Mexico's presidential elections can serve as an indicator of their level of access to political participation and incorporation. For migrants, the vote is the simplest and most direct method for influencing the political system (Calderón Chelius 2003: 31). The electoral system has traditionally been an integrative control mechanism in Mexican politics. Migrants are helping to transform Mexico's politics by demanding participation, pluralism, and representation. Because they maintain binational ties and can stimulate binational political processes, they have the potential to spearhead Mexico's democratization process. And because Mexican migrants constitute an increasing share of the

---

[1] As Leticia Calderón Chelius observes, "Migrants have passed from having only social, cultural, and economic ties with their communities of origin, and have become, in some cases, influential political actors" in Mexico (2003: 219).

U.S. population, they also have the potential to influence political processes in the United States.

This chapter examines the political attitudes and behavior of migrants based predominantly in the United States and compares them with those of nonmigrants and experienced migrants who now reside mainly in Mexico. We discuss voter participation and the Mexican absentee vote, and explore perceptions regarding naturalization as U.S. citizens. Finally, we summarize the determinants of migrants' political participation.

VOTER PARTICIPATION

The right to vote abroad, which expatriates were able to exercise for the first time in July 2006, gives U.S.-based migrants a political voice in their home country and enhances their relationship with political groups in Mexico, giving them a political power of their own (Mummert 1999: 331). The question is not whether Mexicans who reside abroad have the right to vote, but rather what mechanisms are needed for them to easily exercise this right in Mexican elections (Ross Pineda 1999: 119). In addition to enabling migrants to influence political processes in their home country, the absentee vote serves as a symbol of their ties to Mexico, ties that extend beyond cash remittances. As the coordinator of the Mexican Coalition for Mexicans Abroad explained: "we want to vote because it is a basic right of all citizens. For a long time we have sent money to Mexico; now we want to send votes" (Ross Pineda 1999: 122–23).

A national survey conducted in February 2005 by Parametría (2005) found that 54 percent of Mexicans believe their countrymen who reside abroad should be able to vote in Mexican federal elections. This broad public support for absentee balloting was a factor in the Mexican Congress's approval in mid-2005 of legislation that implemented *"el voto remoto"* for the following year's presidential election (McCann, Cornelius, and Leal n.d.). It also demonstrates that Mexicans in general view migrants living abroad as part of the nation and do not consider their residence outside of national territory a barrier to political participation.

Especially since President Vicente Fox championed the migrants' cause beginning in his campaign for the presidency in 2000, the Mexican government has become a proponent of increased political participation by U.S.-based migrants. President Fox declared repeatedly that giving Mexicans abroad the right to vote would be a huge advance in perfecting Mexico's democratic society. In part, this advocacy is a simple recognition that migrants send home more than US$24 billion annually, making them a constituency of great interest to the Mexican government. Jonathan Fox has noted:

> Many immigrants remain engaged in Mexican politics from afar.... In response, the Mexican government has paid a great deal of attention to Mexican immigrant associations, using its extensive network of consular offices to create semi-official channels for growing cross-border participation (Fox 2004: 498).

In 1990 Mexico's Foreign Ministry created the Program for Mexican Communities Abroad (PCME), which promotes the formation of migrant associations organized by state of origin and develops social and economic projects in Mexico with the collaboration of transnational migrants (Bakker and Smith 2003: 65). The PCME is a clear effort on the part of the government to tighten and institutionalize its relations with migrants.

Yet little has been done to develop the economic, political, and social infrastructure needed to boost voter participation among U.S.-based migrants. In the 2000 and 2006 Mexican presidential elections, the migrant vote had little impact. This partly reflects the fact that most Mexicans in the United States do not have a valid Mexican voting credential. To get one, a migrant must apply in person in his or her hometown office of the Federal Electoral Institute and then wait four to six weeks for the credential to be processed (Fitzgerald 2004: 537). In an attempt to facilitate voting for Mexican expatriates, sixty-four special voting booths were set up in Mexican border cities for the 2000 elections. But despite these efforts, Marcelli and Cornelius (2005: 23) report that only 15 percent (7,200) of the ballots recorded in these *casillas especiales* in 2000 are believed to have been cast by expatriate voters. In 2006, while expatriates could vote in the presidential race without returning to Mexico, the procedure for obtaining and casting an absentee ballot was cumbersome, costly, and time-consuming, and migrants lacking a valid voter credential were again excluded. Only 33,131 actually voted absentee, representing 0.06 percent of Mexico's registered voter population and 0.46 percent of the Mexicans of voting age who were believed to be living in the United States at the time of the July 2, 2006 election (McCann, Cornelius, and Leal n.d.).

Results from our 2005 survey show that only 14.1 percent of migrants who were primarily based in the United States at the time of the survey voted in 2000, compared to 63.0 percent of Mexico-based respondents.[2] We would expect residence in Mexico to positively influence the likelihood of voting, for two reasons: Mexico-based individuals could vote more easily, and they are more directly affected by election outcomes. The low participation rate for U.S.-based migrants in 2000 could suggest that they have little incentive to be involved in Mexican electoral processes, but it can also be explained by the difficulties involved in returning to Mexico to vote and then recrossing the border into the United States. Undocumented migrants in particular may be unwilling to vote if it means risking apprehension and expulsion from the United States. In other words, U.S.-based migrants may well value their economic stability over political participation.

Our 2005 survey included several questions regarding a person's intention to vote in the 2006 Mexican presidential election; these questions sought to determine whether U.S.-based migrants can be considered a strong potential political constituency. Our results demonstrate that a significantly larger percentage of both U.S.-based and Mexico-based respondents intended to vote in 2006 than actually voted in 2000. This finding can be attributed in part to Mexico's enhanced political transparency following a reform of the electoral process; Mexicans may believe that elections are more democratic now and, in consequence, feel more enthusiastic about voting. However, our interviews were conducted seven months before procedures for obtaining and casting an absentee ballot in the 2006 election were announced; hence our respondents may have had an unrealistic view of the ease of voting from abroad.

---

[2] $N = 424; p < .001.$

Our results further indicate that more of our Mexico-based respondents intended to vote in 2006 than did our U.S.-based respondents: 88.4 percent of Mexico-based interviewees stated that they intended to vote in 2006, versus 45.7 percent of U.S.-based migrants.[3] Nevertheless, nearly half of our U.S.-based migrants expressed an intention to vote in 2006. Moreover, a much higher fraction of U.S.-based migrants indicated an interest in voting in 2006 if the process could be made less cumbersome. Three-quarters of migrants currently based in the United States said they would vote in 2006 if they did not have to travel back to Mexico to do so. Again, our interviewees were unaware of the actual procedures they would have to follow to vote absentee.

Although procedural obstacles have been cited most often as the explanation for low voter turnout among U.S.-based migrants in 2006, we must also consider the possibility that U.S.-based migrants are simply not strongly interested in Mexican politics. It is to be expected that a person will be most concerned with the politics of the country in which he or she resides, and our findings indicate that this is the case (see figure 9.1): Mexico-based respondents were much more likely than U.S.-based respondents to be interested in Mexican politics (62 versus 16 percent), while U.S.-based respondents were more likely than Mexico-based respondents to be interested in U.S. politics (40 versus 16 percent). Looking exclusively at U.S.-based migrants, we found that those who have legal status in the United States are more likely to be interested in U.S. politics, while undocumented migrants tend to show more interest in Mexican politics. This result is to be expected; legal migrants show more interest in U.S. politics because their status allows them access to economic, social, and political benefits, benefits that are denied to undocumented individuals (see table 9.1).

---

[3] N = 417; $p < .001$. Results from a 2004 survey of 1,514 adults of Mexican origin in the United States conducted by the newspaper *Reforma* are consistent with our findings on migrant intent to vote in Mexico's 2006 elections. The *Reforma* survey found that 59 percent of Mexico-origin U.S. residents had an interest in voting in the 2006 Mexican elections, and that those who have resided less than twenty years in the United States are the ones who show the strongest interest in voting in Mexico's elections (Moreno 2005: 104).

Figure 9.1. Locus of Migrants' Political Interest, by Country

Migrant Political Interest by Country

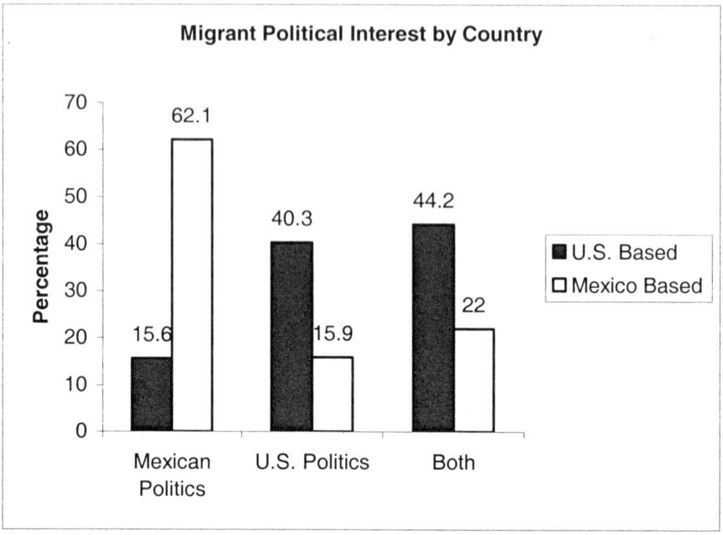

N = 418; *p* < .0001.

Table 9.1. Political Interest among U.S.-Based Migrants, by Legal Status

Migrants Expressing an Interest in:	Legal Migrants	Undocumented Migrants
Mexican politics	12.7%	30.0%
U.S. politics	40.5%	26.7%
Both Mexican and U.S. politics	46.8%	43.3%

N = 141; *p* = .059.

An interesting finding is the large fraction of U.S.-based migrants who are interested in *both* U.S. and Mexican politics, a pattern that holds regardless of legal status (see figure 9.1, table 9.1). These migrants' strong interest in both political systems suggests that they have the potential to assume a binational political identity and a transnational political role. According to Smith and Guarnizo (1998: 201), "migrants can create meaningful transnational political and social life spanning two societies, sovereign territories and political systems." As Carlos, a 58-year-old migrant who has lived in San Diego for the past forty years, explained, "U.S. politics affect Mexican politics."

U.S. CITIZENSHIP

Seeking U.S. citizenship is a second element that, along with electoral participation, can be used to gauge Mexican migrants' political incorporation in the United States. Catherine Bueker (2005) considers citizenship and voting to be the primary components of U.S. political incorporation. Of course, a migrant need not become a naturalized U.S. citizen to have legal status; permanent residency, a temporary visa, and a work permit also enable a migrant to reside legally in the United States. However, as migrants naturalize as U.S. citizens, they can expand their political incorporation in the United States through voting. With voting rights, migrants can form political communities capable of influencing the U.S. political system (and, to a degree, the Mexican political system) as well as the distribution of social and economic resources within and between the two countries (Bueker 2005: 107).

The majority of migrants whom we interviewed expressed a desire to acquire U.S. citizenship—80.6 percent of U.S.-based migrants, versus 65.4 percent of respondents currently based in Mexico.[4] And over 90 percent of both U.S.-based and Mexico-based respondents maintain a positive impression of Mexicans who do naturalize as U.S. citizens. Despite this overwhelming social acceptance of people who become citizens of the United States, some of our interviewees lamented that those who acquire citizenship do not take full advantage of their new political power. Leonor, a former union leader from Tlacuitapa who currently works in a cannery in Watsonville, California, explained: "There are many people who become citizens because of the benefits or in order to help their family members acquire legal status. But they do not have the mind-set needed to care about voting."

---

[4] N = 171; p = .024.

DETERMINANTS OF EXPATRIATE VOTING PARTICIPATION

Recent studies have examined the impacts of various factors on expatriate voter behavior. Marcelli and Cornelius (2005) conclude that individual demographic factors and human capital characteristics have a relatively weak influence on whether an expatriate Mexican voted in the 2000 election or intends to vote in 2006. They argue that:

> institutional constraints rather than individual characteristics have a larger effect on expatriate Mexican voter participation and choice in Mexican elections, and that altering these institutional constraints could yield a significant increase in participation.... Socioeconomic integration into the United States, cross-border mobility, and being affiliated with a political party were more important determinants of whether an expatriate Mexican residing in Los Angeles County voted in the 2000 Mexican election than more conventional individual demographic and human capital characteristics (2005: 14, 26).

Marcelli and Cornelius show that crossing the border less frequently and being undocumented significantly reduced the probability that a migrant voted in the 2000 elections. They also fiind that party affiliation and educational attainment are highly correlated with voting participation. Finally, they find that migrants who demonstrate an intention to vote in 2006 are more likely to have a party affiliation, be male, have earned a high school diploma, be married, have attended at least one religious event, and have legal documents. In addition:

> speaking English well, having resided more years in the United States, having been employed and expecting to be residing in the United States in 2006 are negatively associated with the intent to vote in the 2006 Mexican elections (Marcelli and Cornelius 2005: 15).

In another recent study, Bueker also concludes that education, income, and length of time in the United States affect the likelihood that migrants will both vote and seek citizenship (2005: 132).

Using data from our 2005 study, we ran a regression to assess the impact of various factors on intent to vote in 2006. The independent variables in our model are age, gender, marital status, education, command of the English language, tendency to send remittances, interest in Mexican politics, and 2000 voter participation. The dependent variable is dichotomous and was coded 1 if the respondent reported the intention to vote in 2006. The results of our model are summarized in table 9.2.

Table 9.2. Variables Affecting U.S.-Based Migrants' Intention to Vote in 2006

Variable	Coefficient	Standard Error	Significance
Age	−.011	.025	.647
Male	**1.610**[*]	.829	.052
Married	−.635	.580	.274
Education	**−.242**[*]	.126	.054
English proficiency	**−1.032**[**]	.468	.028
Sends remittances	**.856**[*]	.503	.089
Interest in Mexican politics	**1.085**[**]	.546	.047
Voted in 2000	**2.181**[**]	1.043	.037
Intercept	.829	1.645	.614

Statistically significant at the 95% (**$p < .05$) and 90% (*$p < .10$) confidence level. N = 98. Excludes naturalized citizens of the United States.

We find that, contrary to the results of Bueker, Marcelli, and Cornelius, the more education a migrant has received, the *less* likely he or she is to vote in the 2006 presidential election. One possible explanation for our divergent finding may be that, within our sample, migrants with more education are more likely to naturalize as U.S. citizens and thus are less likely to participate in elections in Mexico. Another consideration is that the highest level of schooling available in Tlacuitapa and Las Ánimas is *secundaria* (grades 7–9), which may have affected the correlation between likelihood of voting and education level in our research communities.[5]

---

[5] A very small percentage of the interviewees in Tlacuitapa and Las Ánimas had attended *preparatoria* (grades 10–12). Fewer than 7 percent of the U.S.-based migrants had attended high school, and only 5 percent had received a college education or higher.

More than 85 percent of our migrant interviewees reported that they understood at least some English, and our regression analysis shows that the more English a migrant understood, the *less* likely they intended to vote in 2006. Migrants with a greater command of English may be more fully assimilated into U.S. society and therefore cognitively less involved in Mexican politics. They may also have adopted U.S. natives' attitudes toward electoral participation, which tend toward nonparticipation, especially if the costs in terms of time and effort are non-trivial.

Our analysis also reveals that immigrants who send remittances to their families in Mexico are more likely to vote in 2006. According to Marcelli and Cornelius (2005: 17), "it is reasonable that one who remits has a greater desire to vote in home-country elections (perceiving a personal or familial stake in government decisions affecting the quality of life in their hometowns)." They find that sending remittances has a positive effect on voting intentions for the 2006 elections, while having sent remittances in 2000 is negatively associated with having voted in the 2000 Mexican election. Fitzgerald notes that "appeals to migrants to invest in Mexico and to maintain a high volume of remittances open spaces for migrants to demand political rights such as absentee voting" (2000: 107). María, a 60-year-old naturalized U.S. citizen who decided to move back to Tlacuitapa, offered the following observation:

> I consider myself an "original" wetback because I went to the United States in the late 1940s. I was four years old when I crossed the Rio Grande on my father's back. I worked in agriculture for over thirty years, always sending money back to my family when I could. When I retired, I decided that I wanted to return to Mexico because I always felt a connection to my birth country. I was blessed that I had a chance to live in the United States and become a U.S. citizen, but I had a sense of *orgullo mexicano* [Mexican pride] in me.... The year 2006 will be my first chance to vote in a Mexican presidential election. I am very excited to vote for the first time in my birth country.

Our results also indicate that there is a significant gender difference in the determinants of intent to vote in 2006, with a male migrant being five times more likely to vote than a female.[6] This gender gap could be partially attributable to differences in the connectedness of migrants to their home community, with women tending to maintain stronger ties.

Finally, our results suggest that migrants who are more interested in Mexican politics are more likely to vote in 2006, and that migrants who voted in 2000 are more likely to vote in 2006. We hypothesize that migrants who are more interested in Mexican politics would be more likely to vote in 2006 because the electoral outcome would have a direct impact on their family members who currently reside in Mexico and an indirect impact on themselves in the United States. Moreover, migrants who voted in 2000 could be more likely to vote in 2006 simply because voting begets more voting; that is, voting can be regarded as an established behavior.

CONCLUSION

> *Mexico's government is very corrupt. It is of no use to any of us because it does not help the people. The bad guy always wins. The government is made up of drug traffickers.*—Zakarías, a 65-year-old ex-bracero who now lives in Jalisco.

> *I do not like the Mexican government. All political parties are hypocrites. They do not fulfill their promises. They take the money and then they forget about the people. I have always hated politics.*—Alejandro, a 23-year-old legal U.S. resident who lives in Oklahoma City and works in construction.

> *I see in the media that [Mexico City] Mayor Manuel López Obrador has done many projects in the capital—huge projects that no mayor had done before. If he ran for president, I would vote for him. I am not from his party; I have never*

---

[6] The odd-ratio of a logistic regression can be calculated by multiplying the exponential function to the power of the coefficient. In this case, $e^{1.610} = 5.003$.

> *liked being from one single party because candidates are made, not born.*—Francisco, a 34-year-old migrant who resides in Jalisco.

The statements of Zakarías and Alejandro, above, reflect the widespread disillusionment in Mexico about the effectiveness of government, while Francisco's words represent the nascent optimism and sense of political power that is growing among Mexicans, inspired by recent changes in the country's political system. This increased optimism appears to extend to Mexicans living abroad. Vicente Fox's election as president of Mexico in 2000 was historic—the first time in over seventy years that the dominant Institutional Revolutionary Party (PRI) lost control of the presidency. Fox's election signaled to the Mexican people that their votes were finally being counted accurately. While the confidence of some may have been shaken by the intensely disputed 2006 presidential election result, national postelection polling data suggest that Mexico's electoral institutions weathered the storm.

The conclusions that we draw from our survey of migrants from Tlacuitapa and Las Ánimas are relevant to the ongoing debate in Mexico over how to incorporate Mexican migrants more fully into their home country's political process. Specifically, we find that:

- Migrants based primarily in the United States are most likely to be interested in *both* U.S. and Mexican politics, indicating their potential ability to play a binational political role.

- Migrants based in the United States were more likely to vote in 2006 if: they voted in 2000, sent remittances home, and had an interest in Mexican politics or in both U.S. and Mexican politics.

However, another of our findings suggests the limits of future migrant participation in home-country elections: a majority of our migrant interviewees expressed a desire to become U.S. citizens. The determining factor in naturalization may be access to the economic, social, and political benefits that accrue to persons with this status. If they follow through with U.S. citizenship, these migrants will be unavailable for voting on the Mexican side of the border.

References

Bakker, Matt, and Michael P. Smith. 2003. "El Rey del Tomate: Migrant Political Transnationalism and Democratization in Mexico," *Migraciones Internacionales* 2 (January–June): 59–83.

Bueker, Catherine S. 2005. "Political Incorporation among Immigrants from Ten Areas of Origin: The Persistence of Source Country Effects," *International Migration Review* 39, no. 1: 103;nd40.

Calderón Chelius, Leticia. 2003. *Votar en la distancia.* Mexico: Instituto Mora.

Fitzgerald, David. 2000. *Negotiating Extra-Territorial Citizenship: Mexican Migration and the Transnational Politics of Community.* La Jolla, Calif.: Center for Comparative Immigration Studies, University of California, San Diego.

———. 2004. "'For 118 Million Mexicans': Emigrants and Chicanos in Mexican Politics." In *Dilemmas of Political Change in Mexico*, edited by Kevin J. Middlebrook. London: Institute of Latin American Studies, University of London and Center for U.S.-Mexican Studies, University of California, San Diego.

Fox, Jonathan. 2004. "Assessing Binational Civil Society Coalitions: Lessons from the Mexico-U.S. Experience." In *Dilemmas of Political Change in Mexico*, edited by Kevin J. Middlebrook. London: Institute of Latin American Studies, University of London and Center for U.S.-Mexican Studies, University of California, San Diego.

Marcelli, Enrico A., and Wayne A. Cornelius. 2005. "Immigrant Voting in Home-Country Elections: Potential Consequences of Extending the Franchise to Expatriate Mexicans Residing in the United States," *Mexican Studies*, Summer.

McCann, James A., Wayne A. Cornelius, and David L. Leal. n.d. "Absentee Voting in 2006 and the Potential for Transnational Civic Engagement among Mexican Expatriates." In *Mexico's Disputed Election: Issue Emergence and Democratic Consolidation in 2006*, ed. Jorge I. Domínguez and Chappell Lawson. Forthcoming.

Moreno, Alejandro. 2005. *Nuestros valores: los mexicanos en México y en Estados Unidos al inicio del siglo XXI.* Mexico: Departamento de Estudios Económicos y Sociopolíticos, BANAMEX.

Mummert, Gail. 1999. *Fronteras fragmentadas.* Morelia, Mich.: El Colegio de Michoacán.

Parametría. 2005. "Encuesta nacional sobre el voto para mexicanos en el extranjero." México, D.F.: Parametría, February, http://www.parametria.com.mx.

Ross Pineda, Raúl. 1999. *Los mexicanos y el voto sin fronteras*. Culiacán Rosales, Sin., México, D.F., and Chicago: Universidad Autónoma de Sinaloa, Centro de Estudios del Movimiento Obrero y Socialista, and Salsedo Press.

Smith, Michael Peter, and Luis Eduardo Guarnizo. 1998. *Transnationalism from Below*. New Brunswick, N.J.: Transaction.

Standardized Questionnaire for Survey of Tlacuitapa, Jalisco, and Las Ánimas, Zacatecas, January 2005

Empleo y residencia durante 2004

1. ¿Cuántos años tiene Ud.?
2. ¿Es usted casado(a) o soltero(a)?
3. ¿Cuántos hijos tiene?
4. ¿Cuántos nacieron en México, y cuántos en los EE.UU.?
5. ¿Hasta qué año llegó Ud. en la escuela?
6. ¿Asistió a la escuela en México, o en los EE.UU.?
7. ¿Qué clase de escuela asistió en los EE.UU.?
8. Durante los últimos 12 meses, ¿a qué tipo de trabajo se dedicó usted, *principalmente?*
9. ¿En qué lugar hacía ese trabajo?
10. En el tiempo que pasó aquí en Tlacuitapa (o Las Animas) durante el año pasado, ¿a qué se dedicaba?
11. ¿Maneja usted terrenos en Tlacuitapa, o cerca del pueblo?
12. ¿Maneja terrenos ejidales?
13. Si es que sí. en total, ¿cuántas hectáreas maneja?
14. ¿Cuántas son de riego?
15. ¿Cuántas hectáreas sembró usted el año pasado?
16. ¿Qué cultivos sembró?
17. ¿Tiene vacas? ¿Cuántos?
18. ¿Usted (o su familia) es dueño de esta casa?
19. Durante los últimos 12 meses, ¿por cuánto tiempo ocupó la casa?
20. ¿Dónde vive Ud. la mayor parte del tiempo: en Tlacuitapa (Las Animas), o en los EE.UU.?
21. Si vive principalmente en EE.UU. ¿qué tan seguido viaja a Tlacuitapa (Las Animas), durante un año regular?
22. ¿Sus visitas a Tlacuitapa (Las Animas) son más o menos seguidas *ahora* que en años anteriores?
23. ¿Por qué? ¿Cuál es la razón más importante?

24. ¿Sabe Ud. inglés? ¿Cuánto?

25. ¿Es necesario entender, hablar, o escribir inglés *para hacer el trabajo* más *reciente* que Ud. hacía (hace) en los EE.UU.?

Historia migratoria de la familia, 1995-2005

26. De *todas* las personas que <u>vivían</u> en esta casa en <u>1995</u>, ¿cuántas **ya no** viven aquí?

27. De las personas que vivían en esta casa en 1995 pero *ya no* forman parte de este hogar, ¿en donde viven ahora?

28. En total, ¿cuántos familiares tiene Ud. que viven actualmente en los EE.UU.?

Historia migratoria del entrevistado e intenciones de emigrar

29. En total, ¿cuántas veces se ha ido a trabajar en los EE.UU.?

30. ¿Cuando fue su *primera* temporada de trabajo en los EE.UU., y cuánto tiempo duró allí? ¿Y su segunda temporada? ¿La tercera? ¿La cuarta? (etc.)

31. Antes de que usted se fue a los EE.UU. *por primera vez*, ¿tenía parientes ya viviendo en los EE.UU.?

32. ¿A dónde llegó a trabajar, en este viaje?

33. En este primer viaje a los EE.UU., ¿pudo pasar con papeles, o tuvo que entrar sin papeles?

34. Si entró <u>con</u> papeles. ¿con qué tipo de papeles?

35. Si entró <u>sin</u> papeles, o con papeles chuecos, ¿qué tan difícil fue, pasar al otro lado?

36. ¿Lo agarraron en la línea, o no? ¿Cuántas veces?

37. En esta *última* temporada en los EE.UU., ¿se quedó más tiempo de lo que había esperado?

38. ¿Por qué fue a los EE.UU., esta última vez?

39. En el mes en que se fue a los EE.UU. esta última vez, ¿tenía algún trabajo aquí en México?

40. ¿Diría Ud. que fue a los EE.UU. *principalmente* para dejar las condiciones de México, o por las oportunidades que ofrece los EE.UU.?

41. Durante esta *última* temporada en los EE.UU., ¿a qué tipo de trabajo se dedicaba usted, la mayor parte del tiempo?

42. ¿En qué lugar hacía ese trabajo?

43. ¿Cómo es que escogió ese lugar en los EE.UU.?

44. ¿Cómo consiguió ese trabajo?

45. ¿Qué tipo de documento le pidió el patrón para conseguir ese trabajo?

46. En este viaje *más reciente* a los EE.UU., ¿pudo pasar con papeles, o tuvo que entrar *sin* papeles?

47. Si entró <u>con</u> papeles, ¿con qué tipo de papeles?

45. Si entró <u>sin</u> papeles, o con papeles chuecos, ¿tuvo que usar coyote, o entró sin coyote?

49. Si <u>no</u> usó coyote, ¿cómo logró cruzar la frontera, sin usar coyote?

50. Si usó coyote, ¿cómo logró conseguir el coyote?

51. ¿Cuánto le pagó?

52. ¿El coyote cumplió con todo lo que prometió?

53. En total, ¿cuánto dinero tuvo que juntar para hacer este viaje a los EE.UU., incluyendo el transporte?

54. ¿Cómo logró juntar el dinero para hacer este viaje?

55. ¿Qué clase de transporte usó Ud. para llegar a la frontera?

56. ¿A qué parte llegó para cruzar la frontera – en cuál estado, o cerca de qué ciudad?

57. ¿Cuánto tiempo tardó su caminada?

58. ¿Su experiencia de cruzar la frontera fue lo que había esperado antes de dejar Tlacuitapa (Las Animas)? ¿Fue más fácil? ¿Más difícil?

59. ¿En qué sentido?

60. Antes de irse a la frontera, ¿había escuchado o había visto algún anuncio sobre los peligros de cruzar la frontera?

61. Si es que sí, ¿esto afectó su decisión de irse, de alguna manera? ¿Cómo?

62. Al intentar a cruzar la frontera, ¿sufrió algún daño físico? ¿Fue robado o asaltado?

63. ¿Lo agarraron en la línea, o no?

64. Si fue agarrado, entonces, ¿cuántas veces intentó cruzar la frontera, antes de poder lograrlo?

65. ¿Recibió algún tipo de maltrato o abuso por las autoridades mexicanas o norteamericanas, o por "vigilantes" norteamericanos, durante este viaje a los EE.UU.? ¿Qué tipo de maltrato o abuso?

66. Si está casado/divorciado/recientemente viudo, durante su estancia más reciente en los EE.UU., ¿estaba su esposa(o) con Ud.?

67. Si es que sí, ¿la(o) acompañó al cruzar la frontera, ya estaba del otro lado, o llegó después?

68. Si tiene hijos, ¿sus hijos e hijas estaban con usted en los EE.UU., durante esta última temporada?

69. Si es que sí, ¿lo(s) acompañó(aron) en cruzar la frontera, o ya estaba(n) los hijos al otro lado?

70. Por qué regresó usted de los EE.UU., esta última vez? ¿Cuál es la razón más importante?

71. ¿Ha pensado en irse a los EE.UU. a trabajar en *este año*? ¿Regresa al mismo trabajo en EE.UU.?

72. ¿Por qué piensa irse?

73. ¿Qué tipo de trabajo piensa tener en los EE.UU., la próxima vez que se va?

74. ¿Por qué ese tipo de trabajo?

75. ¿Este trabajo será arreglado por algún pariente o amigo que ya vive en los EE.UU., o usted tendrá que buscarlo?

76. ¿Cuánto piensa que va a ganar en ese trabajo?

77. Si no piensa irse al norte este año, ¿por qué *no*?

78. ¿Sabe algo, o ha escuchado, de los esfuerzos de la Patrulla Fronteriza para dificultar la entrada de los indocumentados por San Diego, Arizona, y algunos lugares en Tejas?

79. Cómo se enteró de estos esfuerzos de la Migra?

80. ¿Qué tan difícil es evadir la Migra al cruzar la frontera, hoy en día?

81. ¿Por qué cree que es así?

82. ¿Conoce Ud. a alguien que se fue a los EE.UU., pero que se desanimó y se regresó a su pueblo, porque lo había agarrado la Migra en la frontera?

83. ¿Conoce Ud. a alguien que se ha quedado en los EE.UU., en vez de regresar a México, a causa de la vigilancia en la frontera?

84. Actualmente, ¿qué tan *peligroso* es cruzar la frontera, si no tiene papeles?

85. ¿Conoce Ud. a alguien que se fue a los EE.UU. pero al intentar cruzar la frontera, se murió en el desierto o las montañas?

86. ¿Sabe algo, o ha oído hablar, de la propuesta del Presidente Bush para trabajadores migrantes?

87. ¿Qué es lo que propuso el Presidente Bush?

88. En la propuesta de Bush, ¿cuánto tiempo puede permanecer en los EE.UU., la persona que logra conseguir un permiso de trabajo?

89. ¿Qué es lo que tiene que hacer una persona para legalizar su estancia en los EE.UU. bajo la propuesta de Bush?

90. Si el Congreso de los EE.UU. aprueba la propuesta de Bush, ¿es más probable que Ud. se vaya a los EE.UU. a trabajar, o no tiene ningún efecto sobre sus intenciones?

91. ¿Conoce a personas que han ido a los Estados Unidos en los últimos 12 meses, *principalmente* para aprovechar la propuesta de Bush?

92. Actualmente, ¿qué tan difícil es *conseguir trabajo* en los EE.UU., para un mexicano que no tiene papeles?

93. ¿Piensa Ud. que es *más difícil* o *más fácil* conseguir trabajo <u>ahora</u> en los EE.UU. que en <u>años anteriores</u>?

94. ¿Cómo se entera Ud. de cómo está la situación económica allá?

Trabajo y vida en los EE.UU.

95. Durante su trabajo más reciente en los EE.UU., ¿el patrón le pidió algún documento de identificación?

96. Si es que sí. ¿qué tipo de documento?

97. Durante su última temporada en los EE.UU., ¿recibió (recibe) su sueldo por la semana, por la quincena, o por mes?

98. Durante este viaje *más reciente (o actual)* a los EE.UU., ¿mandaba (manda) dinero a sus parientes en México?

100. ¿Para qué se usó este dinero?

101. Cuando regresó a Tlacuitapa (Las Animas) esta última vez, ¿trajo algo de dinero que gastó (o piensa gastar) en el pueblo?

102. Durante su última estancia en los EE.UU., ¿tenía (tiene) cuenta bancaria en ese país?

103. Durante esta estancia en los EE.UU., ¿pagó Ud. impuestos por el dinero que ganó en los EE.UU.?

104. Durante esta temporada más reciente (o actual) en los EE.UU., ¿tuvo hijos en las escuelas?

105. ¿Recibió usted o algún miembro de su familia atención médica en un hospital o una clínica?

106. ¿Quién pagó?

107. ¿Ha sufrido alguna herida o enfermedad relacionada con su trabajo en los EE.UU.?

108. Durante su temporada más reciente en los EE.UU., ¿recibió usted alguna vez "el desempleo"?

109. ¿Recibió usted o algún miembro de su familia "food stamps"?

110. ¿Recibió usted o algún miembro de su familia "el welfare"?

111. Cuando se encuentra en los EE.UU., ¿participa Ud. en algún grupo de mexicanos y/o tlacuitapeños? ¿Cuál?

112. Cuando Ud. está en los EE.UU., ¿cada cuándo se pone en contacto con sus familiares en México?

113. ¿Cómo se mantiene en contacto con ellos, principalmente?

114. Durante su estancia más reciente en los EE.UU., ¿en qué tipo de casa vivió (vive)?

115. ¿Sus vecinos eran (son) mexicanos o norteamericanos?

116. ¿Qué ha sido lo más difícil para usted, de vivir en los EE.UU.?

117. ¿Ha sido discriminado en los EE.UU. por ser inmigrante?

118. ¿Dónde preferiría educar sus hijos, en México o los EE.UU.?

119. ¿Por qué piensa así?

Opiniones sobre su pueblo

120. En su opinión, ¿la migración de gente de aquí a los EE.UU. ha beneficiado o ha perjudicado *la economía* de Tlacuitapa (Las Animas)?

121. En su opinión, ¿la migración de gente de aquí a los EE.UU. ha beneficiado o ha perjudicado *las costumbres y el ambiente moral* de Tlacuitapa (Las Animas)?

122. En su opinión, ¿qué sería necesario para que *menos* gente se fuera de este pueblo, para trabajar o vivir? ¿Cuál es la razón *más* importante?

123. En su opinión, ¿qué es lo que *más* impide el mejoramiento de la producción agrícola y ganadera en este pueblo?

124. Algunas personas dicen que una persona joven, nacida aquí en este pueblo, puede progresar en la vida *sin salir* del pueblo. Otras personas dicen que para superarse, una persona joven nacida aquí *tiene que cambiarse* a otra parte. ¿Qué piensa Ud.?

Situación económica

125. En relación a *hace 5 años*, ¿Ud. y su familia viven mejor ahora, igual, o peor?

126. En relación a su situación actual, ¿cómo cree que van a vivir Ud. y su familia, *dentro de 5 años*?

127. Durante los *últimos 12 meses*, ¿Ud. diría que la situación económica en México ha mejorado o ha empeorado?

128. ¿Ud. diría que *dentro de 12 meses* la situación económica en México mejorará o empeorará?

129. ¿Cree Ud. que el *Tratado de Libre Comercio* ha beneficiado o ha perjudicado a personas como Ud.?

130. Aquí tiene una escalera de 10 escalones. En el número "10" está una familia con las mejores condiciones de vida en este pueblo actualmente. En el número "1" está la familia con las peores condiciones de vida. ¿En cuál escalón se ubicaría Ud. y su familia, actualmente?

Planes para el futuro

131. ¿Está pensando Ud. en irse a vivir a otra parte, permanentemente?

132. ¿A dónde piensa ir?

133. ¿Por qué quiere ir a ese lugar en vez de otro?

134. ¿Cuál es la razón más importante por la cual Ud. no se ha ido a ese lugar todavía?

135. (Si vive actualmente en los EE.UU.), ¿Hay alguna razón por la cual volvería a vivir en México *permanentemente*?

136. (Si estaba "sin papeles" durante su última temporada en EE.UU.), ¿Piensa arreglar sus papeles para quedarse en los EE.UU.?

137. (Si era residente permanente legal durante su última temporada en EE.UU.), ¿Le gustaría hacerse ciudadano norteamericano?

138. ¿Cuál es su impresión de los mexicanos que se hacen ciudadanos norteamericanos?

139. ¿Le interesa *más* lo que pasa en la política de <u>México</u> o en la política de los <u>EE.UU.</u>?

140. (Si <u>no</u> es ciudadano norteamericano), ¿Piensa votar en las elecciones para presidente de México, en <u>2006</u>?

141. ¿Votaría en las elecciones de 2006 si no tuviera que viajar a México para votar? Si podría votar en algún Consulado Mexicano, o por correo?

142. ¿Logró votar en las elecciones mexicanas, en el año <u>2000</u>?

143. ¿Quisiera agregar algo más sobre los temas que hemos tocado?

Guide for Semi-Structured, Life History Interviews with Persons Having U.S. Migration Experience

Historia Migratoria

¿Quién fue el *primer* miembro de su familia que se fue a los EE.UU. a trabajar o vivir?
> ¿Por qué se fue esta persona a los EE.UU.?
> ¿A cuál lugar llegó? ¿Por qué ese lugar?
> ¿Tenía parientes o amigos ya viviendo en los EE.UU.?
> ¿Cuánto tiempo se quedó en los EE.UU.? ¿Regresó a Tlacuitapa? ¿Por qué?

Hablando de *Ud.*: ¿Desde que edad pensaba en irse a los EE.UU. a trabajar? -- ¿Pensaba en irse cuando era niño?

Cuando Ud. se fue a los EE.UU. por primera vez, ¿fue una decisión *propia* o *familiar*?

(Si ha intentado a cruzar la frontera sin papeles, durante los últimos 10 años:) Hablando de su experiencia más reciente cruzando la frontera, ¿intentó cruzar la frontera solo, o con otras personas? ¿Con cuántas? ¿Eran parientes?

¿Cómo les fue en el viaje? (¿Y qué pasó después?)

¿Cómo lo trató el coyote? ¿Entregó todo los servicios que le había prometido?
(Si usó varios coyotes en el mismo viaje:) ¿Qué hizo cada coyote?

¿Hubo algún momento en que se arrepintió de su decisión de cruzar la frontera como indocumentado?
Después de cruzar la frontera, ¿con qué medios contaba Ud. para continuar su viaje a su destino final?

(Si fue detenido por la Patrulla Fronteriza:) Cuando los agentes de la Migra lo detuvieron, ¿cómo lo trataron? ¿Qué es lo que observó y vivió Ud., dentro del edificio donde fue detenido?

Con todo lo que conoce, y todo lo que le pasó en su último intento de cruzar la frontera, ¿volvería a hacerlo otra vez? ¿Por qué?

Experiencias en los EE.UU.

¿Cómo lo han tratado sus patrones en los EE.UU.? ¿Alguna vez se sentía explotado o maltratado por un patrón de allá?

En su lugar de trabajo más reciente en los EE.UU., ¿hay posibilidades de superarse – de conseguir un trabajo mejor? ¿Qué es lo que necesita para avanzar?

¿Ha sido miembro de algún sindicato en los EE.UU.? -- ¿Cuál sindicato? En alguna ocasión durante todo el tiempo que Ud. ha pasado trabajando en los EE.UU., ¿llegaron agentes de la Migra a su lugar de trabajo, para averiguar si los empleados tenían papeles? *(Si la respuesta es sí:)* Cuénteme qué sucedió.

¿Aprendió Ud. algo en su trabajo en los EE.UU. que le ha servido en su trabajo *aquí*? ¿En qué sentido?

Durante su temporada más reciente en los EE.UU., ¿asistía a misa? *(Si la respuesta es sí:)* ¿La gente de la iglesia lo apoyaron de alguna manera?

¿Cuál ha sido su experiencia *más feliz* en los EE.UU.? ¿Y su experiencia *más triste*?

¿Cuál es el problema o la dificultad más grande que tiene, cuando se encuentra en los EE.UU.?

¿Qué es lo que hace allá, durante su tiempo libre?

¿Tiene amigos allá quienes son *norteamericanos*? ¿Qué tan difícil es hacerse amigo de una persona nacida en los EE.UU.? ¿En dónde o cómo los encuentra?
(Si no tenía papeles durante su última temporada en los EE.UU.) ¿Qué tan difícil es vivir en los EE.UU., para una persona que no tiene papeles?

¿Cree que sus experiencias en los EE.UU. han cambiado su manera de pensar o actuar? ¿Cómo?

¿Alguna vez se ha enfermado o se ha lastimado cuando estaba en los EE.UU.?
(Si la respuesta es sí:) ¿Cómo consiguió la atención médica? ¿Estuvo en el hospital? ¿Cómo lo trataron? ¿Quién pagó la cuenta? *(Si no tenía papeles:)* ¿Tuvo dificultades en conseguir atención médica, por no tener papeles?

Algunas personas piensan que en los EE.UU. hay poco respeto por los migrantes mexicanos y mucha hostilidad hacia ellos. Otros piensan que no – que un mexicano trabajando en EE.UU. recibe el respeto que merece. ¿Qué opina Ud.?

¿Por qué cree Ud. que hay norteamericanos que no desean la presencia de inmigrantes dentro de sus ciudades?

Migración y la vida familiar

Cuando Ud. se ha ido a los EE.UU. a trabajar, por lo general, ¿cómo se mantenía su familia aquí? ¿Trabajaba su esposa? ¿Sus hijos? ¿En qué?

Hablando de todas sus temporadas en los EE.UU., ¿cómo han afectado su vida familiar?

(Si tiene hijos:) ¿Sus hijos han estado viviendo con Ud. en los EE.UU.?
(Si la respuesta es sí:) ¿Cómo les va en la escuela de allá?

¿Sus hijos hablan inglés muy bien? ¿Hablan español muy bien?

¿Le gustaría que sus hijos estudiaran en los EE.UU., o en México? ¿Por qué?

(Si es soltero:) ¿Prefiere formar una familia en *México* o en los *EE.UU.?* ¿Por qué?

Impactos de la migración sobre su pueblo

Según lo que Ud. ha visto, ¿las personas que se van a los EE.UU. a trabajar son *diferentes* a los que nunca salieron? ¿Cómo?
Parece que *la mayoría* de la gente en este pueblo se va a los EE.UU. a trabajar. ¿Por qué cree Ud. que *el resto* de las personas no se van al norte también?

¿Qué piensa Ud. sobre las personas que van al norte?

¿Cuáles son los efectos *económicos* de la migración a los EE.UU., en este pueblo?

Si no hubiera tanta emigración al norte de este pueblo, ¿cuáles serían los efectos en Tlacuitapa?

¿Cuáles son los efectos *culturales* de la migración en este pueblo?

En su opinión, ¿los migrantes tienen o deben de tener algún papel en el desarrollo de este pueblo? ¿Qué papel deben de tener?

¿Qué ha aprendido en los EE.UU. que pueda ser útil para el desarrollo de su pueblo?

¿Ha pensado Ud. en poner algún negocio aquí en Tlacuitapa?
(si la respuesta es no:) ¿Por qué no?
(si la respuesta es sí:) ¿Qué tipo de negocio? ¿Qué es lo que hace falta para ponerlo?

¿Tendría interés en juntar algo del dinero que Ud. y otros tlacuitapeños ganan en el otro lado, para hacer alguna mejoría o poner un negocio en el pueblo? *(Si no:)* ¿Por qué no?

¿Conoce usted alguna organización de paisanos en los EE.UU.?
(Si la respuesta es sí:) ¿Los paisanos son de Tlacuitapa, o de otras partes de Jalisco?
¿Qué es lo que hace esta organización? ¿Ha tenido algún cargo en esta organización?

¿Sabe Ud. si hay líderes políticos u oficiales de esta área que han visitado a los paisanos en EE.UU.? *(Si la respuesta es sí:)* ¿Para qué cree Ud. que sirven estas visitas?

Participación política

¿Ha ocupado Ud. algún puesto de gobierno en este pueblo? *[pide detalles]*
¿Cree Ud. que las personas que se van a los EE.UU. a trabajar pueden llegar a ocupar un puesto político o de gobierno, después de regresar de los EE.UU.? ¿Por qué piensa así?

Ud. me dijo en la primera entrevista que le interesa más lo que pasa en la política [mexicana/norteamericana]. ¿Por qué le interesa más la política [mexicana/norteamericana] que la política [norteamericana/mexicana]?

Durante *todas* sus estancias en los EE.UU., ¿alguna vez regresó a México para votar en las elecciones? *(Si la respuesta es sí:)* ¿Cuántas veces? ¿Cuándo fue esto?

Hay una propuesta de que los mexicanos que viven en los EE.UU. tengan derecho a votar en las elecciones presidenciales mexicanas, sin tener que regresar a México. ¿Qué opina Ud. de esta propuesta?

¿Ud. votaría en las próximas elecciones mexicanas, si *no* tuviera que viajar a México para votar?

Hay una ley que dice que un mexicano puede tener otra nacionalidad mientras sigue siendo nacional mexicano. Por ejemplo, puede ser nacional de México **y** Estados Unidos a la vez.
¿Qué opina Ud. de esta ley? ¿Ud. solicitó la doble nacionalidad? *[sí o no:]* ¿Por qué?

(Si no es residente permanente legal o ciudadano de los EE.UU.) ¿Qué tan difícil sería para Ud., conseguir su "tarjeta verde" o residencia permanente en los EE.UU.? ¿Por qué?

¿Ha solicitado una *matrícula consular* de algún consulado mexicano en los EE.UU.?
(Si la respuesta es sí:) ¿Qué tan difícil fue conseguirla? ¿Para qué le ha servido?
(Si la respuesta es no:) ¿Por qué no?